St. Ignatius of Loyola

ST. IGNATIUS OF LOYOLA
In God's Service

Peggy A. Sklar

Paulist Press
New York/Mahwah, N.J.

COVER ART AND INTERIOR ILLUSTRATIONS BY PATRICK KELLEY

COVER DESIGN BY LYNN ELSE

Library of Congress Cataloging-in-Publication

Sklar, Peggy A.
    St. Ignatius of Loyola : in God's service / by Peggy A. Sklar ; illustrated by Patrick Kelley.
      p.   cm.
    Includes bibliographical references (p.).
    ISBN 0-8091-6688-7 (pbk.)
    1. Ignatius of Loyola, Saint, 1491–1556—Juvenile literature. 2. Christian saints—Spain—Biography—Juvenile literature. [1. Ignatius, of Loyola, Saint, 1491–1556. 2. Saints.] I. Title: Saint Ignatius of Loyola. II. Kelley, Patrick, 1963– ill. III. Title.

BX4700.L7 S57 2001
271′.5302—dc21
[B]

                                             00-049574

Published by Paulist Press
997 Macarthur Boulevard
Mahwah, New Jersey 07430

www.paulistpress.com

Printed and bound in the
United States of America

CONTENTS

*To my students
at Holy Trinity Church, Washington, D.C.,
who assisted me in
finding God in all things*

St. Ignatius' Prayer for Generosity

Lord, teach me to be generous.
Teach me to serve you as you deserve,
to give and not to count the cost,
to fight and not to heed the wounds,
to toil and not to seek for rest,
to labor and not to ask for reward,
save that of knowing that I do your will.
Amen.

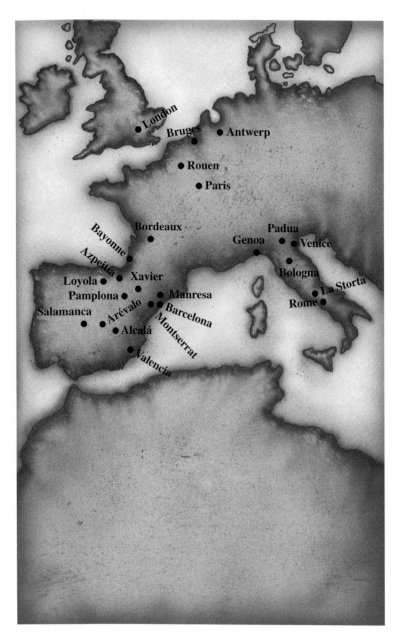

Significant Sites in the Life of Ignatius of Loyola

CHAPTER ONE
THE INVITATION

For many Spaniards, the last decade of the fifteenth century provided new hopes and opportunities for the future. In 1492, Spain would recapture Granada from the Moors who had invaded the country in the eighth century. The conquest of this kingdom would reunite Spain. Perhaps supported by the success of this endeavor, that same year Christopher Columbus's fortunes were reversed. After years of refusal, he was finally granted approval to sail westward to what he thought would be the Orient. His three ships were filled with Spaniards who, like Columbus, sought adventure and wealth. However, in spite of the promise that the time held, it was also a period of religious conflict as Spain sought unity within its borders.

It was into this world that the youngest Loyola, Iñigo, was born to Doña Marína Sánchez de Licona and Beltrán de Oñaz in 1491, at the family's castle. Located in the countryside, the castle was near the small town of Azpeitía. From the grounds of his home, Iñigo could look out at his family's expansive property. The young Iñigo especially enjoyed the apples and chestnuts from their abundant orchards. The nearby Izarraïtz mountains and Urola valley provided both a scenic view and privacy for the family.

Iñigo was a Basque from the mountainous province of Guipúzcoa in northern Spain. The Basques were a proud people with a long history and their own language. Iñigo and his family spoke Euskera, which is today the oldest European language still in existence. Like many families, the Loyolas also spoke Spanish.

As an infant, Iñigo was baptized Iñigo López de Loyola at San Sebastián de Soreasu, the parish church in Azpeitía. He was named Iñigo for the popular Saint Iñigo, an eleventh century abbot of a monastery sixty miles away. The Basque saint had achieved fame for his ability to bring peace as well as rain to the region. López was a common name among members of Iñigo's family. In the Basque tradition, he was named Loyola after the family's castle and land. In a strange quirk of fate, Iñigo also shared his first name with Iñigo Arista, the ninth century first king of Navarre, an independent kingdom in the Pyrenees mountains on the Spanish-French border. Navarre would be important not only to King Iñigo, but to Iñigo de Loyola as well. However, it would be many years before a connection would be made between the two. And it would be many more years before he would become known as Ignatius of Loyola. Much was to happen to young Iñigo before both his life and his name were to change.

As was customary, the infant Iñigo was cared for by a wet nurse, the wife of the local blacksmith. Their stone cottage was a short distance from the Loyola castle. When Iñigo was old enough to return to his family, he discovered a home full of siblings. There were thirteen children in all. Because Iñigo's mother died when he was very young, he turned to his large family for comfort and companionship.

With so many Loyola children, Iñigo knew it was unlikely that he would become lord of the family's castle. According to law, the Loyola land would pass on in its entirety to the heir rather than be divided up into smaller properties for each of the children. Iñigo would have to find another way to support himself.

Some of Iñigo's six older brothers were soldiers who had fought in many of the skirmishes and battles that occurred frequently. Columbus's first voyage to what turned out to be the New World heightened interest in adventure and exploration. Many Basques had sailed on the Santa María. Iñigo's brother, Hernando, liked adventure and would travel to America in just a few short years. As Iñigo contemplated his own future, he knew there were risks involved in many of these choices. His oldest brother, Juan, had died in 1496, battling the French for the Kingdom of Naples. Another option Iñigo had to consider was whether he was called to serve God and the church as a priest like his brother Pero. Iñigo quickly dismissed the idea of pursuing higher education since he had never really enjoyed his lessons. He could read and write, which seemed just fine enough for him.

Fortunately for Iñigo, he was born into a wealthy family. His family had lived in northern Spain for centuries and was not only financially secure, but had many important connections. The family had strong ties to both the government and the church. These connections would be useful in his future plans.

Iñigo's father received a letter from a friend, Don Juan Velázquez de Cuéllar, whose wife, Doña María de Velasco, was a distant relative of Iñigo's mother. Velázquez held the important position of treasurer to King Ferdinand and Queen Isabella of the Kingdom of Castile. The marriage of the king and queen in 1469 had brought many changes to Spain including the union, a decade later, of the Kingdoms of Aragón and Castile. Wielding enormous power, the two monarchs known as *los reyes católicos,* the Catholic Kings, controlled most of what is modern-day Spain. Iñigo's family had a long history of loyalty to the monarch of Castile, and his father had supported King Ferdinand and Queen Isabella in their succession to the Crown.

The letter which Beltrán received invited him to send one of his younger sons to live with the Velázquez family and to serve the treasurer's household. The invitation was not only a gracious one, but the training and experience would provide excellent credentials for the future. After consideration, Beltrán made his decision. He would send his youngest son. The decision was fortunate for Iñigo, for not only did it resolve his career dilemma, but a short time later his father died, leaving him orphaned.

The sixteen-year-old Iñigo set out on the long journey to the home of the Velázquez family. They lived in the town of Arévalo about two hundred and forty miles away. If Iñigo desired a quieter and less hectic home than his own, he would not find it here. Besides the household staff, there were twelve children evenly divided between girls and boys. As Iñigo soon came to see, there were plenty of activities to keep them all busy. Since Velázquez traveled to different cities, Iñigo was able to travel with him as he accompanied the royal court.

Velázquez's position exposed Iñigo to many influential people. Government and church leaders were frequent guests of the treasurer and his wife. Treated like a member of their own family, Iñigo shared in the rich and opulent atmosphere of the household. The teenager could not have wished for more.

During his decade of service to the Velázquez family, Iñigo acquired important social and practical skills such as proper dress, good grooming, and etiquette. The expensive clothing he wore reflected his social status. Iñigo learned to serve at the table where, at banquets and feasts, elaborate multicourse meals were common. The cuisine reflected some of the foods that had been brought back from the New World. The explorers had discovered fruit and vegetables such as avocados, pineapples, tomatoes, and potatoes, as well as a Mexican poultry called *guajolote,* or turkey. Iñigo especially enjoyed the music and dancing at these feasts.

Horsemanship was another important aspect of Iñigo's training. He learned to properly ride and groom a horse. He also learned penmanship, which required him to practice his writing over and over again so that his letters would be clear and legible. At his employer's beckoning, Iñigo would be drafted to write a variety of correspondence.

Iñigo was an apt student in the Velázquez household. Throughout his life, people would comment on the way in which he carried himself. They noticed that he had a certain air about him. He would credit his demeanor to the training he received during this period of his life.

While much of what Iñigo learned was useful and practical, there were some aspects that were less admirable, and even worrisome. For example, he discovered dueling, gambling, and fighting. In addition, Iñigo's fondness for women earned him a reputation as a ladies' man.

Iñigo's indulgent lifestyle also got him in considerable trouble during a particular visit home to his family. Both he and his priest-brother, Pero, were involved in an incident in Azpeitía against local clergy during carnival time, the period before Lent. The festivities and excesses that occurred were similar to those of today's Mardi Gras. The incident involved the Loyola family's patronage of the parish church, which entitled them to appoint priests. The retiring pastor disregarded the family and chose a successor from among his own family, igniting the controversy. The action taken by Iñigo and Pero was so severe that the authorities sought to prosecute them. Pero was able to free himself from prosecution since he claimed immunity as a cleric. Iñigo tried to do likewise since he had earlier been tonsured. For those who are to become priests, a portion of the head is shaved in a circular shape. However, Iñigo's claims for immunity were rejected by the authorities on the grounds that his hair was not currently tonsured, his lavish clothing was non-clerical, and he was not named in a directory of clergy. While the case dragged on for some time, Iñigo appears to have eventually cleared himself. Years later, he characterized this period in his life as one in which he "let the vanities of the world rule [him]."

While Iñigo seemed to enjoy his stay with the Velázquez family, after a decade of service this chapter of his life was to come to an unexpected end. With the death of King Ferdinand in 1516 (and the earlier death of Queen Isabella in 1504), a new ruler came into power and the treasurer fell out of grace with the royal court. Later that same year, Velázquez suddenly died, leaving Iñigo with neither a position nor plans for the future. His years of loyal service had not gone unnoticed, however. Velázquez's widow, in spite of her own anxieties about the future, assisted Iñigo in securing another position. Giving him two horses, some money, and letters of introduction, she sent him to Don Antonio Manrique de Lara, the Duke of Nájera. The duke was Viceroy of Navarre, the small independent kingdom located on Spain's French border.

An older and more experienced Iñigo began service to the duke. His new position was quite different from his previous one. He performed a variety of duties, depending on his employer's needs, including sometimes serving as a soldier. Although not a professional soldier, Iñigo was called on to mediate disputes and to fight at the duke's command. During a dispute between two cities in his own province of Guipúzcoa, Iñigo was sent as a peacemaker. But when the duke learned that French troops were advancing on Pamplona, the capital of Navarre, he sent word for Iñigo to return. Iñigo brought his brother Martín and other men from the castle as well as the province to repel the French invasion. On their arrival, they discovered that the townspeople, weary of the constant fighting over the disputed kingdom and dreading the consequences of yet another battle, had already surrendered. Believing he was no longer needed, Martín left Iñigo and returned home.

Over the years, Spain and France had repeatedly sparred over this small, but important province. In 1512, Navarre had consented to be under French rule. However, before an agreement could be signed, King Ferdinand vowed to reclaim the land and had his troops seize the capital. By the following year, Ferdinand could claim all of Navarre. To defend his capital, the king fortified Pamplona's walls and built a new fortress. As both he and his French counterpart knew, the battle for the kingdom had not ended.

In May 1521, Francis I, King of France, decided that the time was right to reconquer Pamplona. Armed with a strong militia and weapons, the king believed he could prevail over Spain. Although the Spaniards' numbers and equipment were not as great as those of the French, Iñigo felt that it was important to fight for and support the Spanish right to the land. Loyal to both his country and employer, he had no intention of backing down and disappointing either. As a result, the thirty-year-old Iñigo played a decisive role in the Battle of Pamplona, providing evidence of his leadership skills. Ignoring the opposition of the townspeople and his fellow soldiers, he was able to convince his commander and then the Spanish troops not to withdraw.

Despite Iñigo's tenacity and Spain's best efforts, France ultimately won the battle. On May 20, 1521, Iñigo was severely injured in the struggle when a wall of the fortress was damaged, enabling a French cannonball to enter and strike him. His right leg was badly broken and his left one was also wounded. A short time after this, Spain surrendered. However, the French victory was to be short-lived, for just over a month later Spain would reconquer the province.

The French victors in the May battle were kind to Iñigo, and for several days their doctors treated his wounds. Nearly two weeks later, the injured soldier was carried back by stretcher across the rugged mountain range to his family's castle. The ten-day journey through the rough terrain was hard on the gravely injured Iñigo, who was in severe pain. But the brave soldier lay stoically as his stretcher bearers transported him home.

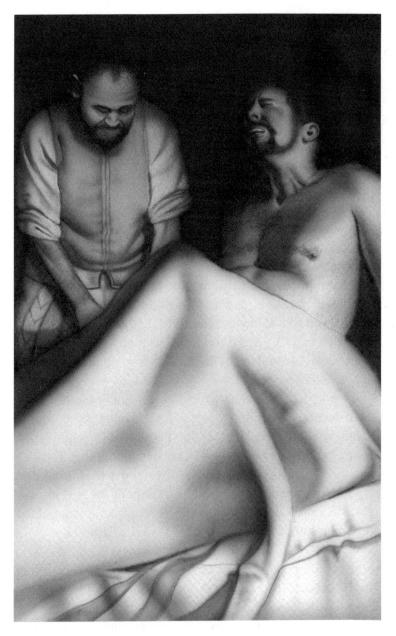

Iñigo endures painful medical treatment for his leg.

CHAPTER TWO
CONVERSION

Iñigo's sister-in-law, Magdalena de Araoz, greeted the fallen hero as he was brought back to the castle. Her husband Martín was away, fighting the French in another battle. Since their father's death, Iñigo's oldest living brother, Martín, and his wife were the lord and lady of the Loyola manor. When Iñigo arrived at the castle, he was warmly received by Magdalena, who quickly summoned doctors to treat his injuries.

The doctors worked hard to stabilize Iñigo's health. They could see he was doing poorly. The treatment rendered by French doctors had not worked or perhaps his condition had worsened because of the difficult journey home. Despite their best efforts, the Spanish physicians thought Iñigo might not survive and advised his family of the seriousness of the situation. Iñigo was given the final sacraments of the church on June 24, the feast of St. John the Baptist.

Iñigo, who had already demonstrated his will and ability to persevere under the most adverse conditions, once again proved that he was a fighter. After praying to St. Peter, he rallied a few days later on the eve of the feast of Saints Peter and Paul. To repair his right leg, he endured the most grueling medical treatments, including the rebreaking of his leg which was performed without the benefit of anesthesia. When it became apparent that his right leg would be permanently shorter than his left, he even endured procedures such as the leg's being stretched, although all these methods were unsuccessful. His will to live carried him through as he lay clenching his fists in pain.

Despite the doctors' efforts, Iñigo's right leg would remain a problem, and he was left with a lifelong limp. For a vain man who prided himself on his appearance and on his ability to attract the attention of women, his injuries caused more than physical discomfort. His self-esteem and pride were wounded as well.

During the long months of his recovery, Iñigo looked for ways to occupy his time. An active person, he was not used to resting and remaining quiet, which would give his body time to heal. To relieve the boredom, he sought out his favorite books. While working in the Velázquez household he had learned to enjoy novels about chivalrous knights. These fictional stories portraying gallant and heroic deeds were very popular at that time. He particularly liked *Amadís de Gaula* (The Prince of Wales) and its sequels. The mythological Amadís could do no wrong, and his supernatural powers made him the envy of many, including Iñigo. He was the "perfect" knight to whom others aspired.

However, to Iñigo's disappointment, none of these books was available at the castle. His sister-in-law could offer him only religious books. His choice was limited to Spanish translations of the four-volume *Life of Christ* by Ludolph of Saxony and the *Golden Legend,* by Jacobus de Voragine, which was about the lives of the saints. As a former lady-in-waiting to Queen Isabella, Magdalena may have brought these books from one of the royal palaces or bought them at auction after the death of the queen. Queen Isabella had compiled a collection of over two hundred and fifty books on a wide variety of topics, which reflected her thirst for knowledge and love of reading. Her collection was especially impressive considering the printing press had only been invented around 1450 in Europe, nearly coinciding with her own birth in 1451. To promote reading, the queen had provided tax relief to Spanish printers and eliminated duties from imported books.

Although these books were far different from those Iñigo had previously enjoyed, he slowly began to read them. As he rested and started to heal, he thought about some of the medieval saints, particularly St. Francis of Assisi (1181/2–1226) and St. Dominic de Guzmán (1170–1221), both of whom he had learned about in his childhood. He wondered if he could become like these holy people.

Similar to Iñigo, St. Francis had come from a privileged background as his father was a successful merchant. St. Francis had enjoyed such a prosperous and carefree life that he was often described as "spoiled" or "wild." However, he turned away from the life he had known to serve God. As a young soldier, he was captured during a war between Assisi and Perugia in Italy and held captive for a year by the Perugians. After his release, he developed a serious illness. When he recovered and was on his way to resume the fighting, he encountered a needy man to whom he gave his clothes. Later Francis became ill again and heard a voice telling him "to serve the master rather than the man." One day he encountered a leper begging alms, and despite the man's visible sores, St. Francis kissed his hand. His concern for the poor and the suffering led him to relinquish everything he owned. He traveled from place to place preaching about God while begging for food and a place to sleep. Others were attracted to St. Francis and his lifestyle, and eventually he established a religious order known as The Order of Friars Minor, or the Franciscans.

Like St. Francis, St. Dominic had devoted his life to helping others. During a famine St. Dominic sold his possessions and gave the money he received to the poor. After experiencing a vision of Saints Peter and Paul, who told him to go out and tell people about God, St. Dominic spent his days preaching in the countryside. He believed he was called by God to lead those who had strayed from the faith back to the church. Education was very important to him and for the religious order he founded, known as the Order of Preachers, or the Dominicans. St. Dominic believed that education should provide the knowledge needed to convey biblical and church teachings accurately, and to refute those who did not teach the truth.

As Iñigo read and reflected on the lives of these saints, he wondered: "What if I, too, were to do what St. Francis did, or what St. Dominic did?" These thoughts were not just the idle fantasies of a sick man pondering the lives of saints. Rather than just admire them and the work they did, Iñigo sincerely wanted to be like them. He told himself, "St. Dominic did this, so I have to do it too. St. Francis did this, so I have to do it too."

Iñigo began to pray and one day, like St. Dominic, he had a vision. Iñigo's vision was of Our Lady, the Virgin Mother, with the Infant Jesus. Over the coming years Iñigo would have many other mystical experiences where he would enjoy a special relationship with Jesus and Mary.

ST. IGNATIUS OF LOYOLA

Still recovering from his injuries, Iñigo began to notice that certain thoughts made him happy, while others provoked unhappiness. He was happy when he thought of making a pilgrimage barefoot to the Holy Land and living like some of the saints. When he thought of the Blessed Mother with Jesus, he was also happy. However, when he thought of more worldly things, such as the life he had led before his injury, he was happy at first, but the happiness did not last. Iñigo was beginning to distinguish which of these thoughts and emotions were from God.

Iñigo's injuries and his experiences during his long recuperation had a profound effect on him, although at the time he may not have been aware of it. Through his readings, reflections, and prayer, Iñigo came to realize that God was calling him to a new life other than serving at court or as a soldier. He was experiencing what is known in the Christian scriptures as *metanoia,* a Greek word that refers to a change of heart or a conversion. For Iñigo, the change was permanent. He gave up all of his old desires in return for a new life of faith and service to God.

What was it that caused Iñigo to change his life? Was it the injury in Pamplona, the lonely months of his recovery, or the books that he read? Can his conversion be attributed to any one thing? In the hectic life that he had led before his injury, there was little time for him to sit quietly and listen to God. But the long months of his recuperation provided him with that opportunity. Was this the first time that God had called Iñigo? Or was it the first time that Iñigo had listened?

His transformation, though highly personal, could not be hidden. His family noticed a change in his demeanor and in his conversation. Besides reading, he also filled numerous sheets of lined paper with his notes, writing the words of

Jesus in red and the words of Mary in blue. Iñigo's family did not know that he had made a life-changing decision, but they could see that there was a certain peacefulness about him. As he continued his readings, he shared with them some of his thoughts on the material he read.

Like many Christians before him, including St. Francis, Iñigo had decided to make a religious journey or a pilgrimage to the Holy Land so that he could trace the steps that Jesus had taken. During Iñigo's lifetime, the Holy Land was one of the three most popular pilgrimage sites to visit. The others were Rome in Italy, as the center of Christianity and the traditional burial place of Saints Peter and Paul, and Santiago de Compostela in Spain, as the traditional burial place of the apostle James who, according to Spanish belief, had been a missionary to Spain. Many Christians traveled to these holy places as a way to gain grace from God, as a church-imposed or self-imposed penance for sins, and even as a punishment for secular crimes. For those unable to travel long distances, there were also numerous local shrines.

When his health finally allowed it, Iñigo made preparations for his journey to the Holy Land. After nine months of recuperation from his injuries, he was anxious to leave the castle. Martín, worried that his younger brother would abandon his career, reminded Iñigo that he need not give up his work. Being a soldier was an honorable profession in the Loyola family, and Martín encouraged Iñigo in this pursuit. Life had changed for Iñigo, though, and he was being led in a different direction. Fighting and valor were not part of his new plans, unless he could be a soldier for Christ. That was a battle Iñigo was willing to consider. But, knowing that his family would not approve of the life he was called to lead, Iñigo chose not to tell them about his pilgrimage.

His brother, Pero, who was now pastor of the parish church in Azpeitía, discovered that Iñigo was planning to leave the castle. He asked Iñigo to accompany him on a visit to one of their sisters who lived in the town of Oñate. Iñigo agreed to do so and, joined by two servants, the brothers departed the family home with their donkeys.

En route to Oñate, Iñigo convinced his brother to stop at a local shrine, Our Lady of Aránzazu. The shrine had been built fifty years earlier after the discovery of a statue of Mary in some bushes. As was the custom, Pero and Iñigo spent the night kneeling in prayer before the altar to Our Lady. In his prayers, Iñigo asked the Blessed Mother to direct his pilgrimage. He also asked for good health during his long journey.

Iñigo parted from his brother at their sister's home and traveled on to see the treasurer of his former employer, the Duke of Nájera, who was now at the town of Navarrete. Iñigo was a hero to the duke, who had been monitoring Iñigo's recovery. The treasurer paid Iñigo the money he was owed for his services. While Iñigo now could have had a job managing one of the duke's extensive landholdings, he was not interested in pursuing this possibility. He used the money he received to pay some of his debts and left the remainder for the restoration of a statue of Mary. Sending his servants home, the pilgrim departed alone on his journey.

CHAPTER THREE
MANRESA

Iñigo's travel plans included a visit to a monastery high in the Catalonia mountains of the town of Montserrat in northeastern Spain. Montserrat, which means "serrated mountain," derives its name from its saw-toothed shape. The town was about thirty miles from Barcelona where Iñigo would later sail for his trip to Italy en route to the Holy Land. As Iñigo approached the mountain base, he stopped at a small town. Entering a shop, he purchased some yards of burlap, which he had made into a sackcloth tunic. He also bought a pair of rope-soled shoes known as *espadrilles.* He only wore one of the shoes, on his right foot, because the leg still had not healed. Other purchases included a pilgrim's staff and a gourd for water. He tied the gourd to the saddle of his donkey and continued his journey.

Three weeks after leaving home Iñigo finally reached the monastery at Montserrat, which had been built by Benedictine monks in the eleventh century. The area drew many pilgrims because of a shrine that was located there. The shrine to Our Lady of Montserrat had been built in the late ninth century after a nearly black wooden statue of Mary and the Infant Jesus was found in a cave. According to tradition, the

ST. IGNATIUS OF LOYOLA

Black Madonna was carved by the gospel writer, Luke, and brought to Barcelona by the apostle Peter. To protect it from Moorish invaders in 717, the statue was concealed in a cave. The statue was discovered by shepherds in 880, who were led to the cave by unexplainable music and scents. The shepherds told a priest and then the bishop, who planned to take the statue to the nearby town of Manresa. However, the statue refused to be moved more than a short distance, so a chapel was built for the Madonna there, drawing thousands of pilgrims to the site each year.

Upon Iñigo's arrival in Montserrat, he sought lodging at a hostel for travelers and then looked for a priest to hear his confession. He spent hours in preparation for the general confession he would make of his whole life. The pilgrim also began shedding many of the symbols of his old life. Imitating St. Francis, Iñigo put on the coarse tunic and gave his fine clothes to a man who had none. Iñigo belted the sackcloth at the waist with a rope. Similar to Esplandían, the son of Amadís in his favorite knight books, Iñigo put down his sword and dagger by the statue of the Black Madonna and knelt all night in vigil at the altar to Mary. No longer needing his donkey, he donated it to the monks to use at the monastery. He would now travel on foot.

Bypassing the road that led to Barcelona to avoid running into people he might know, Iñigo left Montserrat. He began his three-hour walk to the walled town of Manresa located by the Cardoner River. Iñigo sought lodging outside of the town at a hospital for the poor and sick called St. Lucy's. In exchange for a place to sleep on the floor, he assisted in the care of the patients, feeding, bathing, and helping them dress. Iñigo was happy when caring for the sickest among them. Needing to beg alms for food, he frequently walked into town. He later stayed in a room that was offered to him by the Dominican priests at their monastery in Manresa.

During the many months that Iñigo stayed in Manresa, his spiritual life grew. He practiced devotions that he thought would bring him to a closer relationship with God. He sought the sacrament of penance on a regular basis but was still haunted by his past and those things which had caused a separation between himself and God. In frustration, Iñigo prayed aloud, "Show me, Lord, where to find help; and if it is necessary for me to follow a little dog to get help, I shall do so."

In atonement for his past, Iñigo began his practice of severe penances, which over the course of his life would take a permanent toll on his health. He fasted, foregoing the elaborate meals he ate in his former life. Now he begged for his food and subsisted on pieces of bread and water. He declined offers of meat and wine except on Sundays. On one occasion he went without food for an entire week, until his confessor made him stop. He attended daily mass and frequently received holy communion, an uncommon practice at that time.

Iñigo prayed throughout the day at a variety of places. He could be found in prayer at the chapel in the hospital, at the Dominican monastery, or at the stone crosses that dotted the roadsides. In addition, he often took refuge to pray in a shallow cave near the Cardoner River, which actually was an opening in a hill made of stone. It was not unusual for Iñigo to pray on his knees for seven hours a day. The long hours of kneeling increased the pain in his still-healing legs. Despite his discomfort, Iñigo found great consolation in the recitation of the psalms, the daily readings from mass, and scripture passages. He also favored other devotional material such as *The Imitation of Christ,* now attributed to the German priest, Thomas à Kempis. In his popular four-part work, Kempis provides instruction for monks on how they can grow in their following of Christ. During this period, Iñigo developed a lasting devotion to the Holy Trinity and prayed individually to the Three Persons. His thoughts and visions of the Divine Persons often provoked tears.

While in Manresa, Iñigo also began to take notes which eventually were incorporated into a small book known as the *Spiritual Exercises*. The *Spiritual Exercises* are a method of prayer that has been used by Christians to grow closer to God. The stories about Jesus' life that Iñigo had read in *The Life of Christ* during his recuperation at the castle influenced him in writing the *Spiritual Exercises*.

Another outcome of Iñigo's time in Manresa was the pleasure and satisfaction he derived in sharing his faith and beliefs with others. He found that he enjoyed talking to people about God and looked for people with whom he might speak. Later, when he would be accused of teaching without benefit of training or education, he would respond to the charges by describing his talks as conversations between himself and others. There would be many of these "conversations" in the years ahead.

Iñigo's clothing, diet, and lifestyle were no match for Manresa's cold winter. Not surprisingly, he became ill on several occasions. During his long stay, he made the acquaintance of many people, including several women. Once, when he was very sick, he was cared for by some of these women as he recuperated in a room in a private home. They also brought him warm clothes to wear to help ward off the cold and further illness.

Iñigo's voluntary surrender of his clothes, armor, and donkey, months earlier at Montserrat, and the many practices he embraced during his stay at Manresa demonstrated his desire to rid himself of his old life. His expensive and brightly colored garments symbolized his former social status. Since he was no longer the gallant and dashing soldier from the Casa de Loyola, he had no further need for these items. In the new life Iñigo had chosen for himself, he did not want to be burdened by external and unnecessary things.

During these months, Iñigo not only discarded his old garments, but he went one step further and radically altered his appearance as well. He grew his hair long and left it uncombed, and he let his fingernails and toenails grow long and coarse. The careful ways of grooming that he had learned during his time at the Velázquez household were now shunned. Iñigo viewed them as vain and a hindrance in his quest to become closer to God. He modeled himself on a fourth-century Egyptian hermit, St. Onuphrius, who was popular in the Middle Ages. Because of St. Onuphrius's sins, and his desire to seek God, he left his monastery and retreated to the desert. For sixty years he lived in an isolated cave, let his hair grow to his waist, and wore only a loincloth made of leaves. St. Onuphrius wished to follow the Sermon on the Mount, to trust in God, and to seek justice rather than worry about food, drink, or clothes. Jesus had told the disciples: "Seek first the kingdom of God and his righteousness, and all these things will be given you besides" (Matt 6:33).

Despite his startling and unsightly appearance, Iñigo was still able to draw followers. In the years ahead, people from all walks of life would be attracted to him regardless of his looks or mannerisms. Many of these people became his supporters and benefactors, particularly women. Just as women had cared for him while he was ill at Manresa, several would offer him food and money and later contribute to his education, support, and works.

After nearly a year, Iñigo determined it was time to leave Manresa to continue his pilgrimage to the Holy Land. Although he had not planned on staying in Manresa as long as he did, the many months there solidified his plans. The time in prayer and solitude gave him the opportunity to put into practice his new resolve. Freed of his family obligations, he was able to rid himself of anything left of his old life. As he so yearned, he had learned to place his trust in God.

Iñigo began his journey toward Barcelona where he would seek passage to Italy to embark on his pilgrimage to the Holy Land. Others offered to accompany him to Rome, but Iñigo wished to make his pilgrimage alone. He was not deterred by the fact that he knew neither Italian nor Latin. He trusted that God would provide all the company and guidance he needed.

CHAPTER FOUR
PILGRIMAGE TO THE HOLY LAND

In Barcelona, Iñigo looked up his friend, Inés Pascual, one of the women he had met in Manresa. A widow, she lived above her shop near the harbor and offered him a room while he waited for a place on a ship. He continued to fast and pray and often begged for alms. His appearance drew attention, causing people to describe him as *"l'home del sac"* ("the sackman"). During his brief stay in the city, Iñigo continued his habit of looking for people he could talk to about God.

One day as Iñigo sat with some children on steps inside a church, a woman took notice of him. The woman, whose name was Isabel Roser, was struck by the odd man and later told her husband about him. Her description of Iñigo intrigued Señor Roser, and he suggested that she invite him for dinner. After dinner, Iñigo spoke with his hosts about his religious views and shared with them his plans of traveling to Rome. As he did with everyone, he kept his plans of continuing on to the Holy Land private. As a result of the evening, Señora Roser became a friend of Iñigo's and a major benefactor.

Through the help of Señora Pascual, Iñigo was able to secure passage on a ship that was to sail for Italy. Like other pilgrims to the Holy Land, he needed to go to Rome first to obtain papal permission for his journey, which would be granted at Easter. The ship's captain agreed to take Iñigo as a passenger only if he could provide his own food. Content with begging alms, Iñigo did not want to take food. He desired to continue to trust in God's providence. After struggling with the captain's demand and consulting a priest about his dilemma, Iñigo was advised to beg for just the necessary provisions to bring along.

While Iñigo had spent the better part of the past year begging in Manresa, he was not always successful in this activity. Occasionally he met resistance, particularly from those who detected evidence of his past life. His clothes and mannerisms did not always mask his affluent origins or the training he had received so many years earlier at court. In Barcelona, Iñigo received a tongue-lashing from a woman who disapproved of his begging: "You certainly seem to me an evil man, going around the way you do. You would do better to go back to your home, instead of wandering around the world like a good-for-nothing." The agreeable Iñigo merely acknowledged that he was not only a good-for-nothing, but a sinner. His response seems to have met with the woman's approval as she provided him with bread, wine, and other supplies for his journey.

After almost three weeks in Barcelona, Iñigo boarded his ship. He had sufficient food for his trip to Italy and after discovering a few coins in his pocket, he left them on a park bench for someone needier. Five days later, the ship docked at the port of Gaëta, about seventy-five miles south of Rome. Then Iñigo began his long walk to the city. As he came to one walled town, he was forced to sleep in a church because he found the town gates closed due to fear of the plague. He finally arrived in Rome on Palm Sunday at the start of Holy Week, which enabled him to participate in some of the religious observances being held during this sacred time.

In Rome, Iñigo still needed to beg for alms for food while there and for the next leg of his journey. During his stay in the city, he met some Spaniards who tried to talk him out of traveling to the Holy Land. They did not think he would be able to secure free passage. However, Iñigo was determined and would not be deterred from his mission. Obtaining the required papal permission for travel, shortly after Easter, he left Rome for Venice. Pilgrimages to the Holy Land departed from this port city.

As Iñigo neared Venice, he learned that he would be unable to enter the city without a health certificate attesting that he was free of the plague. Seaports such as Venice were particularly vulnerable to the disease since the plague was carried by rodents who either lived near water or were transported by ships. Because Iñigo could not enter Venice, he detoured to Padua where he spent the night in a field. Here he experienced a vision of Jesus, which eased his fears. Iñigo interpreted the vision as a sign of God's support of his pilgrimage. He no longer had to worry that the lack of funds would impede his journey. He knew that God would provide.

Iñigo returned to Venice and, unlike other strangers, he was not stopped, but was admitted without a health certificate. Safely in the city, he now faced his next hurdle. He would have to wait two months before he could secure passage on a ship bound for Cyprus, another stop on the pilgrimage. While waiting, Iñigo passed the time by exploring

Iñigo sails to the Holy Land.

Venice. He continued to beg for alms and after spending the first night in a hospice, he slept outside in St. Mark's Square. One day, Iñigo met a wealthy Spaniard who extended hospitality to him. The Spaniard invited his fellow countryman to his home where Iñigo stayed for several days. In addition, his host made arrangements with the chief official of Venice to secure free passage for him on a ship.

According to the regulations, only one pilgrimage sailing to the Holy Land was scheduled each year. That restriction, coupled with the popularity of pilgrimages, generally produced a large number of travelers. However, this year, 1523, many potential pilgrims were worried about safety and elected not to travel. The preceding December, the Turks had captured the island of Rhodes located off the southwestern coast of Turkey (now part of Greece). Since there were only twenty-one pilgrims waiting to sail, it was too expensive to use the large pilgrim ship. Instead, the group was divided in half and assigned to two merchant vessels. Thirteen of the pilgrims were assigned to one ship, while Iñigo and the remaining seven were selected to sail on the second ship, the *Negrona,* which departed two weeks later than the other one. In addition to the pilgrims on his ship, there were government officials, traders, and merchants.

Just prior to the ship's sailing, Iñigo became seriously ill with a high fever. A doctor was called who advised him against making the trip. He warned his sick patient that he should sail "only if he wished to be buried at sea." After all that Iñigo had endured to get this far, he would not be stopped by illness. He ignored the doctor's advice and ominous prediction and boarded the ship.

Trips of such long duration as a journey to the Holy Land usually required the packing of a great many provisions.

One well-stocked passenger's list included wine kegs, cheese, meat, onions, dried fruit, sugar, salt, eggs, and wooden crates of live poultry. Wine was used because water could not be kept fresh for any length of time. Other items were crockery, goblets, medicines, mattresses, and bed linens. While many of these items were expensive, their costs were often recouped when pilgrims resold them upon their return. The nationality of a ship's passengers could frequently be determined by the diverse scents emanating from the hold of the ships, such as the spices favored by the Italian travelers. Unlike most of the other passengers, Iñigo had no pantry to pack.

After sailing for a month and making three stops, Iñigo's ship finally arrived in Cyprus. Although the pilgrims were supposed to travel on to Beirut, the captain would not sail there because of the plague. Instead, the passengers were forced to walk thirty miles to Las Salinas (now Larnaca) to meet the first ship. Together, the passengers from both ships sailed for Jaffa. Almost six months after leaving Manresa, Iñigo finally arrived at the port of Jaffa in the Holy Land on August 31. In gratitude for having safely reached their destination, the pilgrims joyfully sang two Latin hymns of praise and thanksgiving, *Te Deum* (We Praise You, O God) and *Salve Regina* (Hail, Holy Queen).

In the long months of planning his trip, Iñigo had thought of the many biblical and holy places he would visit. But he had not anticipated the restrictions that authorities placed on the pilgrims. His first disappointment had come when the captain refused to travel to Beirut, forcing the pilgrims to forego the trip to northern Palestine. As a result, Iñigo could not visit Galilee where Jesus had preached and taught, nor Nazareth, the home of Mary and Joseph and where Jesus had been raised. Iñigo was also unable to visit Capernaum, the fishing town where Jesus had healed and taught and where he had called his first disciples. Another restriction placed on the pilgrims was their inability to travel freely. Instead, the visitors were escorted as a group to the sacred sites and resided together at the travelers' hospice of St. John, which had been established for pilgrims.

From the port of Jaffa, Iñigo and the others rode donkeys to Jerusalem. On their first day, a Saturday, they visited this holy city, which King David had made his capital and where his son, King Solomon, had built the Temple. As an infant, Jesus had been brought by his parents to the Temple to be dedicated in accordance with Jewish law. Later, at the age of twelve, he and his parents traveled to Jerusalem for the Passover festival, and when he was thought to be lost, his parents found him in the Temple sitting among the teachers. As an adult, Jesus ministered in Jerusalem, and it is where he was arrested, tried, and crucified.

While touring Mount Zion, in the Temple area, the pilgrims also visited the Upper Room or Cenacle where Jesus had celebrated the Passover with his disciples and instituted the Eucharist at the Last Supper. According to the Gospel of John, it is also the place in which Jesus washed his disciples' feet in an act of humility and service. After the resurrection, Jesus appeared to his disciples in the Upper Room, and it is there that the Holy Spirit descended on them at Pentecost.

The pilgrims next visited the column of the flagellation, which was the site of Jesus's scourging; the column has since been moved to Rome. They went to the convent of the Dormition of Our Lady, which commemorates the death of Mary with a life-sized figure of her asleep. It is near the place from which Mary was taken up to heaven. Iñigo and the others also saw the homes of three of those involved in Jesus's trial and crucifixion: Annas, the former high-priest; Caiaphas, his son-in-law and high-priest; and Pilate, the governor of Judea.

As was customary, the pilgrims spent the night in vigil at the Church of the Holy Sepulchre, which was built over the place of Jesus's death and burial. The pilgrims attended mass and received holy communion in the church. Later that Sunday, they made the Stations of the Cross along the Via Dolorosa (Way of Sorrows). This devotion, marking some of the places Jesus passed on his way to the crucifixion, was established by the Franciscans in the fourteenth century.

The next day the pilgrims visited the villages of Bethany and Bethphage. Bethany was home to Jesus's friends, Martha and Mary, and their brother Lazarus, whom Jesus raised from the dead. According to tradition, Jesus had sent his disciples to Bethphage to obtain the donkey that carried him into Jerusalem where he was greeted by people waving palm branches. Iñigo and the others then traveled to the Mount of Olives, a mountain located to the east of Jerusalem and known for its ancient olive groves. Jesus had prayed at the Mount of Olives the night before he died. Forty days after Easter, he ascended into heaven from a rock there, which still has the imprint of his feet.

The following two days, Iñigo and the others traveled to Bethlehem. In Hebrew, Bethlehem means "House of Bread"; it is located about five miles south of Jerusalem. Jesus was descended from the line of King David and was born in David's city, according to the Christmas stories of the Gospels of Matthew and Luke. Jesus's birth is commemorated by the Basilica of the Nativity.

The pilgrims next toured the valley of Jehosaphat and the brook of Kidron, where Jesus prayed in the Garden of Gethsemane, was betrayed by Judas Iscariot, and was arrested. After resting for two days, the pilgrims went to Jericho and the Jordan River. In Jericho, Jesus cured a blind man and invited himself to Zacchaeus's house, where Zacchaeus experienced his conversion. Seeing the Jordan River, Iñigo was reminded of Jesus's baptism.

The instability of that region was experienced first-hand by the pilgrims when, during their stay, Turkish troops entered Jerusalem. For over a week, Iñigo and the others were forced to stay inside and were unable to visit other holy places. Despite the fear of hostilities as well as the restrictions placed on the pilgrims, Iñigo was grateful that he had made the journey. His trip confirmed his growing desire to stay in the Holy Land and bring Christianity to the Turkish Muslims. While he had once considered joining a Spanish monastery after his pilgrimage, he now felt that he wanted to labor in the Holy Land. However, despite his wishes and the obstacles he had overcome in making the long and arduous journey, Iñigo was frustrated to discover that he could not remain. He would have to leave with the other pilgrims after what had turned out to be a brief visit.

Although safety concerns were not an issue for Iñigo, they were for the Franciscan authorities, who had held responsibility for Christian travelers in the Holy Land since the fourteenth century. As the Muslims now controlled the Holy Land, the Franciscans were wary of pilgrims like Iñigo who might cause conflict and jeopardize the lives of Christians there. In the past, pilgrims had been taken hostage and even killed, and the Franciscans feared having to pay a ransom to secure their release. Threatened with excommunication if he disobeyed the order to leave, Iñigo reluctantly departed with the other pilgrims after their nearly three-week stay. But just prior to his departure, he slipped away to make one last visit to the Mount of Olives. He gave the guards his pen knife in order to be admitted. He desired one final look at the rock from which Jesus ascended into heaven. Besides leaving the group, Iñigo went without taking a guide, which alarmed the Franciscans. They sent a servant waving a staff to retrieve him.

On the night of September 23, the pilgrims left Jerusalem. They again experienced the unstable nature of the region when they were confronted by Arab nomads called Bedouins, who took their food. Then, upon arriving at Ramle, the pilgrims were imprisoned by the Turks for three days and deprived of food and water. Exhausted, the pilgrims finally reached the port of Jaffa and left the following day for Cyprus. Two weeks later, they arrived in Las Salinas. Having come too late to sail on the *Negrona,* they were placed on three other ships. Iñigo was denied a place by the captain on the large Venetian ship. Although the other pilgrims attested to his holiness, the captain was unconvinced and suggested that Iñigo travel with the help of angels, like St. James. (Following his missionary service in Spain, St. James returned to Jerusalem where he was martyred. According to tradition, angels guided the ship carrying his body back to Spain.)

Undefeated, Iñigo finally secured passage on a small vessel free of charge. Due to inclement weather, it took two and a-half months to reach its destination. Despite the snow and cold conditions, the poorly dressed pilgrim persevered. As fate would have it, Iñigo's journey was the most unremarkable of the three. The ship in which he had been denied passage sank, although the passengers were rescued. The passengers on the second ship, a Turkish one, were not as fortunate; they were lost when their ship also sank. Only the small ship that had taken Iñigo arrived unscathed.

After his wearying journey, Iñigo finally reached Venice. He had the good fortune of encountering the man who had provided him hospitality on his earlier trip. The man again showed his generosity by giving Iñigo alms.

Since his initial plan to stay in the Holy Land was thwarted, Iñigo now had to find another way to serve God. As he contemplated what he should do next, Iñigo realized he had made a mistake in not taking his studies more seriously in his youth. He decided that he would remedy that situation by returning to Spain to study. His later desire to be ordained to the priesthood may have taken root then.

The rest of Iñigo's journey back to his homeland was not without incident. One day as he was traveling, he stopped to pray at the Cathedral of St. George in Ferrara. One by one, he was approached by people needing money. Iñigo gave one coin, then another, until finally he had none left. As he continued toward Genoa where he would take sail for Barcelona, Iñigo encountered some Spanish soldiers who pointed out a safer route. Ignoring their advice, he approached one walled town where he was mistaken for a spy and arrested. Stripped and restrained, he was taken by his captives to their captain. Untroubled, Iñigo thought only of Jesus' arrest. In the end, Iñigo was able to disentangle himself from the situation by his disheveled appearance and his speech. To the captain's frustration, Iñigo responded to questions slowly and in one syllable words. The authorities concluded that, rather than a spy, the stranger was a deranged man who posed no threat. Iñigo was freed.

After his release, he encountered a Spaniard who offered him food and a place to spend the night. The next day he continued his journey and was again stopped by two soldiers who took him to their French captain. By chance, the captain was from a Basque province in France not far from Iñigo's own province. He ordered that Iñigo be fed and released.

Once again Iñigo continued walking toward Genoa. When he finally arrived in the port city, he encountered someone he knew from his days of service at the royal court. The man arranged for passage to Barcelona and, at last, Iñigo began his final leg of the journey back to Spain.

CHAPTER FIVE
THE STUDENT IN SPAIN

Shortly after his arrival in Barcelona, Iñigo traveled to Manresa where he sought out a monk he had known during his stay there. Since Iñigo had decided to study, he thought the monk would make a good teacher and might take him on as a student. However, Iñigo soon discovered that since his departure from Manresa, the monk had died. Iñigo then returned to Barcelona to pursue his studies.

He again stayed at the home of his friend, Inés Pascual. Isabel Roser, another of his friends from Barcelona, arranged for him to study Latin with a teacher. At that time, Latin was the language of both the university and the church. Students needed Latin in order to understand lectures and read their textbooks on philosophy and theology.

As had been the case since his days in Manresa, Iñigo continued to attract attention. Once he was physically assaulted by a man who resented his criticism of some nuns. Although those nuns were cloistered, they entertained visitors and left their convent freely. The man's severe beating would not dissuade Iñigo from expressing his views. Later, he would work toward the reform of Spanish religious life, which had grown increasingly lax.

At this time, since he felt physically better than he had in the past, Iñigo returned to his custom of embracing extreme penances. He made holes in the soles of his shoes; eventually only the top parts remained. By winter, he was nearly barefoot.

Besides studying, Iñigo also visited the sick as he had done in Manresa. He began to teach children catechism or religious doctrine. He also gave his Spiritual Exercises to people he thought would benefit from them. He attracted a group of young men to him as companions and they began to follow him in his activities.

As Iñigo studied and read, he was introduced to the works of the Dutch scholar and Christian humanist, Desiderius Erasmus of Rotterdam (1466–1536), an advocate of church reform. A close friend of Sir Thomas More in England, Erasmus was gaining renown, although questions would later be raised about some of his views. Iñigo was given a Latin copy of Erasmus's devotional work, *Enchiridion Militis Christiani (Manual of a Christian Soldier)* to help him in learning the Latin language. The two-part book provides a guide to living a Christian life.

After two years of preparation in Barcelona, Iñigo had made enough progress that he could continue his studies at a more advanced level. The new University of Alcalá was recommended to him. Cardinal Francisco Jiménez de Cisneros, the Franciscan archbishop of Toledo, had founded the university in 1508. The archbishop, like many Europeans of the time, supported reforms in the church and society. After walking four hundred miles from Barcelona, Iñigo arrived at Alcalá. There he planned to study humanities or the liberal arts.

One day as he was begging alms in Alcalá, he was ridiculed by a cleric, who viewed Iñigo's begging as a sign of laziness. The administrator of the local hospital, Our

Lady of Mercy, observed Iñigo's encounter with the cleric. Feeling for the poor man's plight, and perhaps taken by the gentility of his response, the administrator offered him a much-needed room at his hospital. Iñigo accepted the offer.

Iñigo's stay in Alcalá was supposed to be dedicated to his studies. However, he could not refrain from reaching out to other people and talking to them of God. He continued to find people to direct in his Spiritual Exercises as well as children to whom he could teach catechism. His companions from Barcelona also joined him in Alcalá.

Iñigo's desire to study came during the time of the Spanish Inquisition. While many Spanish leaders supported reforms, they also advocated national unity. The leaders were unable to conceive of a pluralistic society where all of Spain's citizens could live harmoniously and worship according to their own beliefs. As a result, Spanish officials sought to unify the country by making all citizens practice one religion, and purging Spain of those groups that would not convert. The Spanish Inquisition was the means for implementing this plan.

The Inquisition had existed in other European countries since its approval by Pope Gregory IX in 1232. When Pope Sixtus IV approved it in a papal bull in 1478, it was instituted in Spain. In contrast to other countries, Spain's government rather than the church was granted control of the Inquisition. Government control enabled the monarchs to appoint their own inquisitors charged with investigating allegations. The inquisitors conducted hearings and assigned punishments ranging from penances to imprisonment, or even death. Although approval for the Spanish Inquisition was granted, there was not total agreement about it. Archbishop Alfonso Carrillo, Cisneros's predecessor as archbishop of the influential see of Toledo, voiced his objection. In 1481, he wrote that conflicts in the church "divide the seamless garment of Christ."

The primary targets of the Spanish Inquisition were Jews and Muslims, who were Moors from North Africa. On March 31, 1492, the government issued an edict giving Jews four months to decide whether to convert or leave Spain. A decade later, a similar order was given to Moors in Castile on February 12, 1502. Many of the Moors elected to convert to Catholicism, while thousands of Jews fled to other lands.

While Jews and Muslims were initial targets of the Spanish Inquisition, other citizens came under suspicion as well. The inquisitors investigated those Christians accused of heresy, or false teaching. Iñigo, who continued to attract notice wherever he went, soon came to the attention of authorities. Questions were beginning to arise regarding his qualifications to teach.

In response to charges that had been brought against Iñigo and his companions, called the "sack wearers," the inquisitors interviewed four witnesses. At the investigation's conclusion, it was determined that Iñigo and his companions were innocent of any wrongdoing pertaining to their lifestyle or teaching. They were informed, however, that they could no longer dress alike in long garments, similar to cassocks or priests' robes, since people might think they were members of a religious order. They were ordered to vary the color of their clothing with some wearing black and others wearing "lion-color" or light brown garments. The group complied with this order. A short time later, Iñigo was informed that he must also wear shoes so he would not to be mistaken for a monk.

A few months later, Iñigo was again investigated. While he was never told why, he thought it might be because of an

Iñigo is once more arrested by the Inquisition.

earlier encounter with a well-known married woman from the community, who had visited him in his room. Three witnesses were called, but nothing came of the investigation.

Four months later, Iñigo was once more arrested. Given no reason for his imprisonment, he was in custody for seventeen days before he was questioned. He finally learned that he was suspected in the disappearance of two prominent local women, a mother and her daughter, along with their servant. He was targeted because he had spoken to the women on numerous occasions regarding their interest in traveling to visit the poor in hospitals. He told his questioners that while he had talked to the women, he had advised them that there was no need to travel as there were plenty of people at home whom they could help. Imprisoned for six weeks, Iñigo was allowed visitors, and some of his friends and supporters wanted to use their influence to free him. He rejected their offer, saying, "He for whose love I entered here will get me out if it be to his service."

Iñigo was finally released when the women returned home and informed the inquisitors that their absence was due to a pilgrimage they had made to a shrine in southern Spain. Iñigo again received instructions about the clothes he and his group wore. They were now told to dress as students. In addition, they were restricted from teaching on religious topics until they had obtained more education. When Iñigo protested that neither he nor the others could afford new clothes, suitable outfits were provided for them.

After his experience with the inquisitors, Iñigo decided that he would leave Alcalá to study in Salamanca. The University of Salamanca was Spain's oldest university, having been established in the thirteenth century. Similar to Alcalá, classes were in Latin, and teachers were fined if they taught in Spanish. Several years earlier, Queen Isabella had employed a woman lecturer from the university to teach her Latin. The remarkable presence of women lecturers at Salamanca as well as at Alcalá may have resulted from the long and powerful reign of the female monarch. The queen viewed education so highly that she saw to it that not only her son, but her four daughters as well, were well educated.

Iñigo finally arrived at Salamanca after a seventy-mile walk and met his companions who were already there. According to his custom, he began conversing with everyone he met in the city. Whether attracted by his appearance or his message, people crowded around him. He also continued his practice of teaching religion to children. Although he had been forbidden to teach in Alcalá, the restriction was not applicable in Salamanca.

Iñigo and his companions may have believed, or at least hoped, that they would not face the problems with authorities in Salamanca that they had in Alcalá. However, their activities soon brought undesired attention to them and particularly to their teaching. Although Iñigo had been in the city less than two weeks, questions were beginning to surface.

One Sunday Iñigo and a companion were invited to dinner by a group of Dominican priests, some of whom taught at the university. The priest who issued the invitation informed Iñigo that his hosts would ask him questions. At the conclusion of the dinner, the Dominicans and their guests went to the chapel where the priests queried Iñigo and his companion about their education and teaching. Iñigo told his hosts about his minimal education and shared with them the topics of his "conversations." Asked what he preached, he responded, "We do not preach, but we speak familiarly of spiritual things with a few as one does after dinner, with those who invite us." Not satisfied with his response, his questioner pressed as to the subject manner. Iñigo told them, "When we see virtues, we praise them; when we see vices, we condemn them."

His responses to his hosts' questions raised a red flag for the learned Dominicans, who could not understand how he or his companions could be teaching about complex matters of faith, considering their lack of education. As a result, the Dominicans detained Iñigo and his companion in the monastery for three days. They were then imprisoned in an unused, rat-infested cell, separated from the other prisoners who were in the dungeon. Chained together to a post, Iñigo and his companion were forced to move in unison. While they were being held, two of the other companions were also arrested but were sent to the dungeon. The fourth companion was allowed to remain free. While their prisoners were incarcerated, the Dominicans took a copy of Iñigo's spiritual notes for review.

During their imprisonment, a jail break took place in the dungeon, and all but the two companions fled. Their lack of flight was recognized and all four prisoners were moved to a mansion where they were held together until the conclusion of the investigation. After twenty-two days of imprisonment, Iñigo was declared free of any errors, and the four were released. He was advised he could resume his activities as long as he did not teach on matters of sin until he had completed his studies. Iñigo agreed to follow the prohibition for as long as he remained in Salamanca.

At the time of his release, Iñigo had been in Salamanca only two months. In that short period of time, he had not had the opportunity to study or fulfill his many plans. He evaluated his situation and concluded that if he remained in Salamanca, he would be unable to teach, and he did not believe he could adhere to that restriction. As a result, he decided to leave not only Salamanca, but Spain as well. His experience with the Dominicans and with the inquisitors in Alcalá had clearly demonstrated the problems he faced if he wished to teach and converse with people about God. From his time in Manresa, he had learned the importance of sharing with others some of the insights he had learned, particularly about matters such as sin. He decided he would move to France where he hoped he would be able to study and teach.

Iñigo's four companions did not accompany him as he left Salamanca. They planned to remain in Salamanca and join him later in France. Shortly after his release, Iñigo returned to Barcelona in preparation for his journey. His friends tried to talk him out of leaving Spain, just as they and others had tried to do when he had left for Rome. They argued that he did not speak French, but Iñigo knew language barriers had not hindered his journey to Italy or to the Holy Land. They would not do so now. Even the threat that the French "roasted the Spanish on spits" was not enough to intimidate him. Iñigo had made his decision and would be deterred by neither language nor conflict.

CHAPTER SIX
PARIS

Accompanied by a donkey that carried his books, Iñigo began his seven-hundred-mile trek to Paris on foot. Despite the cold winter air and snowy conditions, a determined Iñigo walked toward his next destination. He looked forward to a new challenge and the opportunity of studying at the famed University of Paris, a renowned theological center. Its reputation drew students from throughout Europe. Located in the Latin Quarter, which acquired its name from the language spoken in class, the university was comprised of numerous colleges. During his six years in France, Iñigo was associated with three of the colleges—Montaígu, Sainte-Barbe, and the Sorbonne. The Sorbonne held such prominence that the university was often referred to by the college's name.

After his experience in Spain, where he had devoted little time to serious study, Iñigo realized the difficulty of balancing his studies and his interest in helping others. He knew the time he had spent away from his studies had ill equipped him for the scholastic demands required in Paris. He resolved to devote more of his time to study and postpone his efforts toward helping others until after he graduated.

At the age of thirty-seven, much older than most of the other students, Iñigo enrolled at the Collège de Montaígu to study humanities, which included the study of Latin grammar and literature. So that he would not have to beg for alms, Iñigo had been given money by some of his Spanish benefactors. He found a room in a boarding house with other Spanish students and turned over the money he was given to another student there for safekeeping. The student quickly spent the money. A short time later Iñigo learned that he was now without the means to either support himself or pay for his schooling.

Without financial support, Iñigo was quickly forced to change his plans. He left the boarding house and found a room at the Hospital Saint-Jacques, a hospice for pilgrims on their way to the shrine of Santiago de Compostela in Spain. Located away from the school, Iñigo now had to commute, carrying his heavy books and inkpot to campus. He was disappointed that he would not be living with other students or taking his meals with them. In addition, the hospice's hours, which were strictly observed, conflicted with the hours of school, forcing him to miss both his early morning and evening classes. He also was left with far too little time to study with the walk to and from school, his class schedule, and the need to beg alms.

Iñigo, faced with these unforeseen problems, was still trying to adjust to the strict academic life of the university. He had not come from a family that emphasized education, but was instead a self-motivated student seeking education as an adult. In Spain, he had studied with a private tutor in Barcelona and had only attended lectures in Alcalá. In the rigorous program he now faced, students rose at 4:00 A.M. so that they could attend their first class at 5:00 A.M., followed

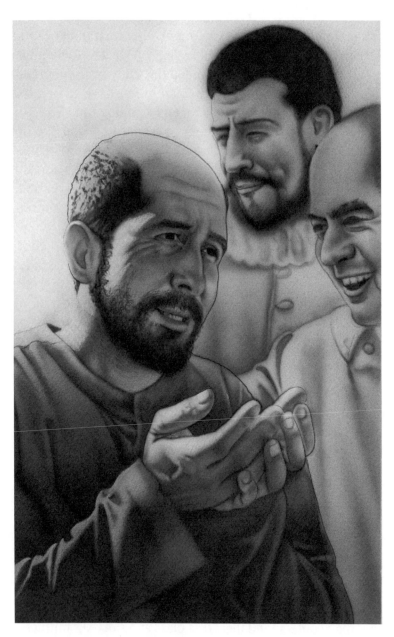

Iñigo begs alms to pay for his education.

by mass at 6:00 A.M. The students then ate a breakfast of bread and water, before their second class, which ran from 8:00 A.M. to 10:00 A.M. Iñigo and his classmates sat in their student gowns on grass or straw on the floor because there were no tables or desks. The teacher stood above them at a lectern. After the morning classes, an hour of disputations followed where, under intense scrutiny, a student had to provide a vigorous defense of an assigned topic that was challenged by other students. Following a light dinner, students read their assigned materials. They were then questioned on the subject matter taught that day and were expected to have mastered it. They attended a third class in the afternoon from 3:00 P.M. to 5:00 P.M., which again was followed by disputations. Supper was served at 6:00 P.M., and an hour later students were questioned once more. They had a curfew of 8:00 P.M. in the winter and 9:00 P.M. in the summer, and had to obtain permission to light candles any later than that.

Struggling with all of the demands placed on him, Iñigo knew that resolving his financial and living problems were paramount to a successful adjustment. He struggled to come up with various options. One possibility was to obtain a position working for a professor in exchange for room and board. However, he was unable to find anyone willing to hire him. A Spanish friar suggested another idea. He proposed that Iñigo leave school for a month and travel to Flanders, which was then part of the Spanish empire, to beg alms. Since many affluent Spanish merchants sold their goods in Bruges and Antwerp, they might be willing to help the indigent student from their homeland. Without a viable alternative, Iñigo decided to try the friar's suggestion even though he would have to leave school temporarily. His first trip was so successful that he was able to move closer to his classes. For the following two years, he returned to Flanders for two-month stays. Each of his trips provided enough alms to support him for an entire year. The last year, he also traveled to London where he succeeded in begging among the Spanish merchants there on business.

As a full-time student, Iñigo now had the opportunity to interact and converse with other men. This was a different experience for him, since he had taught and conversed mostly with women while in Spain. Iñigo gave his Spiritual Exercises to several students and, as often occurred, many of them experienced profound changes. Three of these students taught some of the classes and were known as masters. They came from prominent families and were preparing for university careers. However, after completing the Exercises, they turned away from their career plans. They gave their books and other possessions to the poor. Relinquishing the security that their former life had offered, they now lived day to day, begging for alms.

Even though the masters had decided on their own to change their lives, reaction from the university community was not supportive. The students in their classes were particularly upset, since their courses were not yet completed. The students took their grievances to the school authorities, who blamed Iñigo for the masters' actions. He was threatened with the embarrassment of a public flogging by the head of the college.

While Iñigo was trying to free himself from his latest predicament, he was contacted by the Spanish student who had misspent his money when he had first arrived in Paris. Although left destitute by the student's actions, Iñigo held no ill will toward him. The youth, sick and stranded without money in Rouen, now sought Iñigo's help in returning to

Spain. Iñigo prayed about the youth's request and concluded that if he helped him, he might win him to "God's service." As a self-imposed penance, Iñigo walked the seventy-six miles to Rouen in three days, barefoot and without taking either food or drink. He aided the ailing youth and from his own alms provided the money the student needed to return home. Iñigo also gave him some letters he had written that were for his Spanish companions. Although they had hoped to follow Iñigo to Paris, this plan was never realized.

When Iñigo returned to Paris, he found the fury had not died down about the three masters. The uproar that had resulted had been brought to the attention of the French inquisitor. Iñigo went to him to find out what, if any, charges had been brought. He had not forgotten his experiences in Spain and was determined not to let anything stand in the way of his education. Iñigo was never officially summoned before the inquisitor, suggesting that the matter was dropped.

The students, though, were still furious and had not given up the idea of having their teachers return at least to finish their courses. When they could not convince them to return voluntarily, the students forcefully brought them back. Without being given much choice, the masters then agreed to finish teaching their courses before adopting their new way of life.

Since he had completed his study at Montaígu, Iñigo enrolled in the Collège de Sainte-Barbe to study philosophy. Having enough alms, he moved into a room with three others: a master who would teach Iñigo and two students, the intellectual Pierre Favre and the fun-loving fellow Basque, Francis Xavier, both of whom were much younger than Iñigo. Favre helped Iñigo with his studies and quickly became a close friend. The friendship between Iñigo and

Xavier would take much longer to form. They had to overcome not only a fifteen-year age difference and diverse personalities, but the fact that Xavier's older brothers and Iñigo had fought on opposite sides for the possession of Navarre. Eventually, the three students became good friends.

Just as Iñigo had been successful in attracting a following in Spain, he had no trouble in attracting others to him in Paris. Besides his roommates, he made close friends with four other students—Simón Rodrigues, Diego Laínez, Alfonso Salmerón, and Nicolás Bobadilla. Two of the students, Laínez and Salmerón, were Spaniards, who had heard stories about Iñigo while studying at the University of Alcalá. Over the course of several months, each of the six students made the Exercises with Iñigo and became his companions.

One day, as Iñigo was speaking to a professor, a friar approached and asked for the professor's help in locating another place to stay. The friar had learned that the house where he had a room was infected with the plague. Iñigo, the professor, and a woman with expertise in diagnosing the disease, went to the house, where the woman confirmed its presence. Iñigo went into the home and found an infected person. He comforted the sick man and touched one of his sores, not unlike St. Francis had done three centuries earlier in his encounter with a leper. Later, Iñigo's hand began to ache, and he placed it into his mouth saying, "If I have the plague in my hand, I will also have it in my mouth." When word spread among the students of Iñigo's actions, he was forced to make a hasty exit from his room and classes for a few days.

After finishing his study, Iñigo received his long-awaited Bachelor of Arts degree. Subsequently, he received his licentiate, which allowed him to teach. Following the award of the licentiate, Iñigo registered at the Collège de Sorbonne and with the Dominicans to study theology. At the conclusion of this study, Iñigo earned a Master of Arts degree in theology. He had now completed seven years of study in Paris. Since he did not have enough money for graduation, he had to wait a year to receive his degree. The degree enabled him to teach at any of the colleges of the University of Paris. As was the custom, Iñigo also was given at graduation a four-cornered biretta, which was a special cap worn by clerics.

The master's degree awarded to Iñigo records his name as Ignatius rather than the one given at his baptism. From that time on, he would be known as Ignatius. Although it is impossible to know precisely why, he may have taken the name of the early second-century Christian martyr, St. Ignatius of Antioch. To more closely imitate Jesus, the elderly bishop of Antioch chose death rather than let his supporters free him from captivity.

As the three masters had demonstrated, the Spiritual Exercises often had a profound experience on people. Many who took them responded in some dramatic way, such as giving up material goods or turning away from previous practices and lifestyles. Ignatius's Parisian companions were no different, and after discussion they talked about the future and decided they wanted to stay together. On the Feast of the Assumption of Our Lady, on August 15, 1534 at a secluded chapel dedicated to the Blessed Virgin Mary at Montmartre, Ignatius and his companions made vows. Pierre Favre, who had recently been ordained to the priesthood, presided at a mass in the crypt, during which they took vows of chastity and poverty. Each promised that when he had finished studying, he would travel to the Holy Land, which Ignatius still longed to do. They also pledged that they would wait one year in Venice and if they were unable to make the trip by January 1538, they would go to Rome and offer their services to the Holy Father. They would then go wherever the pope thought they were most needed. They agreed they would meet again in Venice in preparation for their trip to the Holy Land.

While Ignatius had finished his studies, his companions had not. He decided that while he was waiting for them, he would return to Spain. He had recurring stomach problems that often left him in excruciating pain for several hours. He had not responded to any of the treatments recommended by doctors. Having exhausted all remedies, the doctors suggested that Ignatius return to Spain to see if the air of his own country might help him.

As Ignatius was preparing for his trip, he learned that an accusation had been made against him with the inquisitor. Hoping to head off trouble, Ignatius again went to the inquisitor to find out the nature of the charge. The inquisitor dismissed the charge as inconsequential but did request a copy of the notes Ignatius used in giving the Exercises, which he then praised and asked to keep. Wary, Ignatius brought a public notary and some witnesses so that he could have a written record of his clearance.

Ignatius finally left Paris for Spain. It had been thirteen years since he had been home. In the last several years, he had exchanged only one letter with his brother, Martín, who had written to Ignatius after hearing he was in Paris. The two brothers would soon meet again.

CHAPTER SEVEN
A VISIT TO AZPEITÍA

Although Ignatius had decided to return to Spain and to his hometown of Azpeitía, he was determined not to stay at the family castle. He had long ago broken with his old life, and his new life would not afford him the luxury of even sleeping in the ancestral home. Riding the horse his companions had given him, Ignatius made the five-hundred-fifty-mile journey in a month's time. As he came closer to home, he left the main roads and took a more remote route in the hope of escaping notice. To his dismay, he encountered two strangers, not roving bandits as were common, but servants of his brother. Word had spread of his homecoming, and they had been sent to escort him back. However, as his family would soon learn, Ignatius would not change his plans. He was returning to his hometown a far different person from the one who had left so many years ago. Ignatius was making this trip on his own terms.

While Ignatius's family was happy to be reunited with him, they were embarrassed by his lifestyle. He stayed at the Hospital de la Magdalena, one of two hospices for the poor, despite the family's protest. He traded the horse he had been given in exchange for a room. His family sent him a bed and supplies, but they went unused as Ignatius slept on the floor. Each morning he rumpled the bed clothes so that it would look as if the bed had been slept in. The hospice soon discovered his ruse, and the bed was returned to the castle. In return, Ignatius agreed to sleep on one of the pauper's beds. His family had not been prepared for his appearance, which further added to their dismay. The dashing and well-groomed soldier they remembered was a distant memory to Ignatius and one better forgotten in his eyes. Fortunately for his siblings, Ignatius had long ago returned to cutting his hair and nails, sparing them some of the extreme behavior that he had earlier embraced.

In Azpeitía, Ignatius continued the activities he had undertaken almost everywhere he had lived. He begged for alms, which he shared, as he took his meals with the others at the hospice. Each day he taught catechism to children. Martín, unfamiliar with Ignatius's teaching and his success in attracting people to him, predicted that no one would be interested in hearing his brother. Undaunted, Ignatius responded, "If I can teach just one child, then I will have succeeded." For two hours, three evenings a week, he preached on spiritual matters and the scriptures, focusing on several occasions on the Ten Commandments. As in the past, large numbers of adults came to listen, drawing so many people to the hospice that he was forced to move outdoors. Not only townspeople, but residents of surrounding villages and towns came, some to catch a glimpse of the man they had once known, others to see the man they had heard so much about. Unable to find space, some of the vast hordes of people even resorted to climbing trees to get a better view, as Zacchaeus had done when Jesus came to Jericho. Ignatius climbed into a fruit tree himself so he could be seen. On Sundays, the people crowded into the parish church where he was invited to preach.

Ignatius told the people who had come to hear him that he wanted to make amends for some of the wrongs he had committed years earlier. He publicly apologized for a youthful misdeed when, as an adolescent, he and some friends had stolen fruit from trees for which someone else was severely punished. Pointing out the man in the crowd who had borne his wrongs, Ignatius offered him two of the farms that he still owned, one as repayment and the other as a gift. The repentant Ignatius hoped that others would use the opportunity of his visit and his confession to correct their own wrongdoings.

Some of Ignatius's wishes were realized when his preaching against gambling, a vice he knew all too well from his own past, resulted in a three-year abstinence from playing cards and dice among the townspeople. His message was so successful that the local river was soon littered with discarded cards. However, Ignatius was not satisfied with just stopping the practice. He went a step further and sought to outlaw the sale of playing cards entirely.

In another area, Ignatius converted some women from prostitution, and for months people marveled at this. Then he discovered that unmarried girls and women living as concubines were wearing head coverings, as was the custom of married women. Ignatius feared that those living in illicit relationships were confusing people by providing the impression that they had the blessing of authorities. He succeeded in securing the passage of a law which allowed only married women to cover their heads. He even intervened in a long and very public dispute between parish priests and the nearby convent of nuns and mediated a resolution of their conflict.

Care of the poor was another area where Ignatius hoped the townspeople would make changes. He convinced authorities to begin offering some provisions to the needy on a regular basis, so they would not need to beg. The Loyola family added to the town's contribution, as Martín agreed to provide each week twelve large loaves of bread baked at the castle.

Ignatius also introduced the Roman custom of ringing church bells for the Angelus, three times a day in the parish church and shrines, so that the people could pray. To ensure that the practice would continue, Martín left money to pay the ringers in his will.

In addition to his teaching and preaching, Ignatius was sought for his ability to heal the sick. He also earned a reputation for his sensitivity to people and for seeming to know about the future. One day, while Ignatius was teaching some children, a boy was ridiculed for his stuttering. Seeing a teaching opportunity, Ignatius told those assembled that the boy would grow up to serve God, and in fact the boy later became a priest.

Despite the hope that his visit to Spain would cure him of his ailments, Ignatius became seriously ill during his stay. Rejecting offers to move back home and let his family care for him, he was treated at the hospice like one of its own patients. Some of his worried family members stayed and helped with his care, and he recovered.

After three months in Azpeitía, Ignatius determined it was time for him to leave. Despite pleas to stay, he would not be swayed. Once Ignatius had made up his mind, there was no point arguing with him. After leaving home, he stopped briefly in Pamplona, the site of his old war injuries. Wanting to visit the families of some of his Paris companions, he then walked to their old hometowns. Carrying letters, he brought news of their well-being and conducted business matters for them. Some, like Francis Xavier, had not been home in many years. Xavier had left home at nineteen for the University of Paris, knowing he might never see his family again. Ignatius also visited one of his old companions from his time in Spain.

When Ignatius left Spain, it would be for the last time. He still had another year before his planned rendezvous with his companions in Venice. Till then, he decided to go to Italy and continue his studies in Bologna in preparation for ordination as a priest, which was now part of his plans. Despite the usual warnings that it was unsafe to sail, he left from Valencia for Genoa. En route, a terrifying storm broke the ship's rudder. Competing with the howls of the wind and rain were the anguished cries and prayers of the frightened passengers. All aboard feared for the worst.

Surviving their nerve-racking passage, Ignatius and the other passengers arrived in Genoa somewhat scarred, but safe. If his passage weren't memorable enough, Ignatius endured another fright as he made his one-hundred-eighty-mile walk to Bologna. Becoming lost and missing the road, he mistakenly walked along a river bank so swollen that he was forced to crawl on his hands and knees along broken and jagged rocks. In yet another mishap, near Bologna, Ignatius slipped from a footbridge and emerged covered in mud, much to the amusement of the watching townspeople. As if he had not already experienced enough misfortune, he was unsuccessful in begging for alms in Bologna, despite the size and prosperity of the city. Unable to survive without alms and soon becoming sick from the cold, he was forced to give up the idea of studying there. When he was well enough, he left for Venice.

In Venice, Ignatius found a place to stay and soon engaged in spiritual conversations with the people he met. With the closest university in Padua, twenty-three miles away, he abandoned his idea of studying at a university and instead planned to study alone. He continued to give the Exercises, in spite of the fact that rumors were surfacing about them. One recipient, a Spanish priest, Diego de Hoces, had been warned against taking them and was prepared to refute them with his books, if necessary. However, as he soon discovered, the warnings were unwarranted and Hoces was so changed by his experience that he asked to join Ignatius.

CHAPTER EIGHT
REUNION IN VENICE

Although it was still too early for Ignatius's companions to leave Paris for Venice, rising hostilities between France and Spain made them readjust their timetable. Since several of the companions were Spanish, the group decided it was best to leave France. So as not to arouse suspicions in their long school gowns and wide-rimmed hats, they initially divided into two groups but rejoined outside Paris. Walking with their Bibles and their books strapped to their backs, their rosaries around their necks, and holding a pilgrim's staff in their hands, they made quite a sight. To minimize the danger posed by conflict, they were forced to zigzag their way eastward across France. After years of study, the companions looked forward to a new beginning. As they walked, they sang, prayed, and engaged in conversation with people they met, telling questioners that they were making a pilgrimage to a shrine in eastern France.

After trudging through driving rain and deep snow for two months, the companions reached Venice where they were finally reunited with Ignatius. Since Ignatius had left Paris, three new companions had made the Exercises and had joined the group in France. They were Claude Jay and

Ignatius is reunited with the companions.

Paschase Broët, who were priests, and Jean Codure. The three newest companions came from different places in France. If Ignatius had worried during their separation whether his companions would remain united to their mission, he had no need for concern. The companions neither gave up their new-found ways nor relinquished their agreed-upon plans, remaining strongly committed to their ideals. Their commitment was so strong that each year on the August 15 anniversary of their vows, they met at Montmartre to renew them.

For the next two months, while Ignatius continued studying for his ordination, the companions divided into groups and went to work at two local hospitals, including one that cared for people suffering from incurable diseases. The companions toiled among the poor and sick, helping wherever they were needed. They fed and cared for the patients, several of whom shared each bed, lying side by side on huge wooden platforms. Besides helping with patients, the companions made beds, emptied bedpans, swept floors, dug graves, and buried the dead; those who were priests also did counseling and heard confessions. Ignatius hoped that through these duties they would learn service and humility as he had at Manresa.

As Easter approached, the companions began preparations to travel to Rome to obtain papal permission for their trip to the Holy Land. They looked forward to being in Rome for Holy Week and Easter to partake in the religious observances. Ignatius chose to remain behind in Venice, believing there were now two men at the papal court who were unfriendly to him. One of Ignatius's presumed adversaries was Dr. Pedro Ortiz, a relative of one of the French masters who had given up his university career. Dr. Ortiz was in Rome as a representative of Charles V, the Holy Roman

Emperor. The other man was Bishop Gian Pietro Carafa, one of the founders in 1524 of a religious order known as the Theatines. He was shortly to be elevated to cardinal (and in 1555, at the age of 79, would become Pope Paul IV). Carafa and Ignatius held irreconcilable views on many aspects of religious life, including the need for begging, preaching, and practicing corporal works of mercy. Ignatius believed that only by working in the world, engaged in these types of activities, would others be drawn to join them in religious life or at least to support them in their work.

Traveling together, the companions arrived in Rome on Palm Sunday and, much to their surprise, found Dr. Ortiz to be quite helpful to them. Through his assistance, they were able to obtain an audience with the pope on Easter Tuesday. Impressed by what he had heard of these young men who aspired to travel to the Holy Land to work among the Turkish Muslims, the pope invited them for dinner. At the pope's table, the young companions engaged in theological dialogue with the older, more distinguished guests, including members of the papal curia. The pope approved their pilgrimage, placing no limits on the length of their stay, and even joined with others in contributing money for their journey. The companions were warned, though, that the current instability of the region might delay their voyage. They also requested and received the Holy Father's approval of the ordination of those companions who were not already priests.

Having finished their business, the companions left Rome and returned to Venice where they resumed their hospital work. Planning to sail in late spring or early summer, they learned a short time later that travel to the Holy Land was canceled due to impending war. For the first time in nearly forty years, there would be no travel. With few alternatives, the companions decided they would wait until the following year and see if they could then set sail. If they were still unable to travel, they would go to Rome and place themselves at the service of the pope. Not needing the money they had been given, Ignatius returned it to the donors and asked that it be held until the following year.

As they readjusted their plans, Ignatius and five of the companions were ordained to the priesthood in the sacrament of holy orders on June 24, 1538, the feast of St. John the Baptist. Salmerón, the youngest companion, was ordained as a deacon because of his age and would be ordained to the priesthood the following year. Drawing lots, the companions then divided into groups of two and three and went to five different cities in northern Italy where they would spend the next forty days in prayer before saying their first masses.

Ignatius departed with Favre and Laínez for Vicenza, forty-three miles west of Venice. The three stayed in an abandoned monastery. Having lost both its doors and windows, the building offered little protection from the elements. The three men slept on straw that they had brought with them. Devoting most of their time to prayer, they were still in need of alms so Favre and Laínez left twice a day to beg. Ignatius prepared their simple meals when bread was available. After the forty days, they were joined by a fourth companion, Codure, and decided they would begin preaching. Each companion went to a different square of the city and at the same time each day preached, even though none was fluent in Italian. They shouted and waved their birettas for attention, which drew crowds around them. Their language difficulties proved to be of little importance as the people were receptive and gave them alms.

Soon the other companions joined those gathered in Vicenza, with the exception of Xavier and Rodrigues who were ill and unable to travel. The companions had to decide what they would do next. They determined that for the next six months they would break into groups again and travel to Italian universities where they would work among the students. They hoped that after conversing with the students, some might be inclined to join them. Their plan was to teach, preach, give the Exercises, and hear confessions. But before they departed they still had one remaining decision to make: knowing they would attract attention and questions would be raised about them, how would they answer the questions concerning what kind of group they were, or their name? Ignatius's companions had earlier faced these same questions in their journey from Paris to Venice, when people wondered who they were and whether they were priests or monks. After prayerful deliberation, they decided upon a name. They would call themselves after Jesus, since they were working in his service. The name they chose was *Compañía de Jesús.* The word *compañía,* or company, ordinarily referred to a society or association and had no military meaning. In this situation, the word was used to designate a group of friends or associates.

Ignatius and the others learned that while they were away rumors had been spreading about him. He was said to have come to Italy after being burned in effigy in Spain and Paris, which meant that a lifesize dummy of him had been burned in hatred. And as had happened many times before, the rumors quickly aroused the suspicion of authorities. After initiating an official investigation with witnesses, Ignatius was found innocent of any wrongdoing. Cleared, he and the others could now proceed with their plans to leave for the universities.

Ignatius left with Favre and Laínez for Rome, while the others went to Padua, Ferrara, Bologna, and Siena. Since his early concerns about being poorly received in Rome had been unfounded, he felt free to go there. As he and his two companions traveled from Siena to Rome, they came upon a small chapel at the village of La Storta, about eight miles from their destination. Ignatius entered the chapel and, while praying, experienced a vision of God the Father and Jesus. In the vision, God the Father told Jesus to make Ignatius his disciple. Jesus turned to Ignatius and expressed that it was his will that Ignatius serve them. God the Father then promised to look favorably upon Ignatius in Rome. Once again, Ignatius knew he had God's support.

Ignatius and his companions found a vacant house in Rome in which to stay. Collecting donations of food and clothing, they distributed them among the needy. While Favre and Laínez began lecturing at the University of Rome, Ignatius preached and traveled back and forth through the city giving the Exercises. Several prominent people benefited from them, including Dr. Ortiz.

During this period one of the companions, Hoces, died in Padua, and two new men joined the group. By Easter the companions were all in Rome, and they moved to a large house in the center of the city. The only problem with the house was that according to lore it was haunted. Needing a place to stay, Ignatius and his companions were willing to take that risk.

Their plan now was to preach in the different churches in Rome. This plan was short-lived, however, for they soon found themselves under siege. Rumors began surfacing in the city that the group was really Lutheran and was trying to gain adherents through the guise of the Exercises. Ignatius was said to have been in trouble in Alcalá, Salamanca, Paris, and Venice, before retreating to Rome. This time, not only Ignatius but the entire group was suspect. They were accused of leading sinful lives and engaging in heretical teaching.

This latest controversy had its origins in the Lenten preaching of an Augustinian friar who was teaching Lutheran rather than Catholic doctrine. The priest would later leave the church and join Martin Luther's followers. He was challenged by Favre and Laínez, which set off a storm of protest from the friar's friends, including those in the papal curia. Ignatius attacked the accusation in his customary way by confronting it head on. He first went to see a cardinal who was a supporter of the friar. After meeting with Ignatius, the cardinal abandoned his previous support of the friar and favored Ignatius instead. Next, Ignatius went to see the governor of Rome, taking with him a letter from one of his main attackers. In the letter, the writer praised the companions and expressed interest in joining them. The letter writer was a former servant of Xavier's in Paris who had joined the companions, then left. When denied re-admittance, he had become a fierce enemy. The letter pointed to the man's duplicity, and when confronted by the governor he admitted his deceit. Although both the cardinal and governor saw that the charges were groundless, Ignatius asked the governor and papal delegate (the pope was out of the city) for a trial to resolve the situation. Since people were already shunning their preaching and other activities, Ignatius felt that only a judicial decision would enable them to continue their work. Although the accusers backed down at the threat of a trial, Ignatius was firm in his desire to obtain one.

Ignatius next asked for an audience with the pope, Paul III, to pursue his desire for a trial. The pope granted the audience and Ignatius used the opportunity to inform him about the previous accusations made against him. He requested that the Holy Father order an investigation of the current charges so that the matter would be legally resolved. Granting Ignatius's request, the pope ordered the governor of Rome to commence a legal investigation. To Ignatius's good fortune, the individuals who had investigated him in Alcalá, Paris, and Venice were in Rome for various reasons during the course of the investigation and were officially interviewed. Dr. Ortiz also testified on their behalf. The proceeding cleared Ignatius of any false teaching and proved that he and his companions led Christian lives. Once again, accusations leveled against Ignatius were found to be groundless and erroneous.

Enjoying the peace and normalcy that were returning to their lives and work, Ignatius and the others looked forward to their pilgrimage to the Holy Land. The peace at home did not, unfortunately, extend to the region of the Holy Land, and they were again unable to make their journey. Since they had already waited longer than they had planned, the companions knew it was time to place themselves at the service of the Holy Father.

Although Ignatius's companions had celebrated their first masses while they were in Vicenza, he had not. He may have been waiting to do so until he reached the Holy Land. Since their travel was now curtailed, Ignatius said his first mass on Christmas Eve, 1538, in the Chapel of the Manger in Rome's Basilica of St. Mary Major, eighteen months after his ordination to the priesthood. His eyes overflowed with tears as he presided at his first liturgy at the altar which was said to contain a relic of Jesus's manger. From his stay in Manresa, Ignatius's thoughts and visions of the Holy Trinity or the Divine Persons were frequently accompanied by tears. As he wrote in his diary, Ignatius often said mass in honor of the Holy Trinity. His devotion to the Divine Persons was so great that, while preparing for or saying mass, he not only wept but sobbed and even lost his speech. He experienced eye pain from the constant flow of tears.

In the new year, as Ignatius and the others continued their work in Rome, they encountered the extraordinarily cold and bleak winter of 1539. The conditions caused great havoc in the city, including a devastating famine. The companions worked to help as many people as they could, opening their spacious but sparsely-furnished house. They provided physical aid, including food and shelter, as well as spiritual help, engaging in prayer and catechesis. While some of the companions stayed at home to serve and care for their houseguests, others, attired in their long black cassocks, ventured out to collect the much-needed alms. They also sought housing for the many more they were unable to house. In all, the companions assisted nearly three thousand people for a period of several months. As they worked among the blustery conditions of that winter, the companions pondered their own fate. What did the future hold for them? What was God calling them to do?

CHAPTER NINE
A NEW RELIGIOUS ORDER

For several months the companions debated what to do. The pope would soon be requesting their assistance and they needed to make a decision. Should they place themselves at the hands of the Holy Father as individuals or as members of a religious community? After careful deliberation and prayer, they decided they would form a religious community. They had already devised a name for themselves: the Spanish *Compañía de Jesús* (in Latin *Societas Jesu* and, as it became known in English, the Society of Jesus, or the Jesuits). They had taken the unusual step of calling themselves after Jesus rather than after their founder, like other orders such as the Franciscans and the Dominicans had.

The Jesuits differed from other existing religious orders in several other ways as well. It was important to Ignatius that he and his companions work in the world and not away from it in strict prayer and labor, as was common among priests and brothers who lived in monasteries. Ignatius believed that all of life is prayer and that everything that is done is for God. The Jesuit motto in Latin is *Ad Majorem Dei Gloriam* (A.M.D.G.), which means "for the greater glory of God."

Ignatius composed the first "Formula" of the new order similar to the "Rule" found in other orders. Consisting of Five Chapters, the Formula contained the essential elements of the order, including the name; the three vows of poverty, chastity, and obedience, plus a fourth one pledging obedience to the pope; and the requirements for admission of members and their formation. Other components were the authority of the general, who would serve for life; the rejection of property; the private recitation of the divine office, or daily prayers of the church recited at different hours of the day; and penances. After its review by the appropriate officials, the Formula was submitted to Pope Paul III who orally approved it in September 1539. He acknowledged God's role in the order's formation by saying, "The finger of God is here."

The pope's secretary, Cardinal Girolamo Ghinucci, determined that a bull was needed to establish the new order. The issuance of the bull would subject the Formula to further review. The cardinal objected to some of the elements in the Formula, including the private rather than common recitation of the divine office. Ignatius believed that private recitation would be more practical, considering the work of the order, and would also reflect his belief that all of life is prayer. Ghinucci also disagreed with the elimination of the practice of penances imposed by rule, i.e., established by the order. Knowing that his health problems resulted from his extreme penances, Ignatius favored a self-determination of penances, decided in conjunction with a superior. He felt that this approach might eliminate some of the more extreme behaviors he had adopted from the practices of the saints. From his own experiences, he sought to help preserve the health of members. The cardinal also objected to the inclusion of the fourth vow, which reflected the companions' earlier decision to place themselves at the pope's service. Ghinucci believed that since the pope was sovereign over all the faithful, a vow of obedience to him was redundant.

In light of the objections being raised, the pope placed the matter in the hands of Cardinal Bartolomeo Guidiccioni, which presented yet another problem because he did not believe a new order was needed. The cardinal thought there were enough orders in the church, and that religious life should be limited to the Benedictines, Cistertians, Franciscans, and Dominicans. He believed these four orders provided enough variation to satisfy those called to religious life.

Seeing the roadblocks in his path, Ignatius marshaled all of the forces he could to overcome the objections being raised. He prayed and asked his supporters to join him in prayer and to recommend the order's approval by the pope. As many had already learned, when faced with opposition Ignatius could be a formidable foe. Letters of support came from all of the places the companions had served attesting to their good work. In one final measure, Ignatius decided that he and others would offer three thousand masses to the Holy Trinity. The culmination of these efforts (or perhaps the masses) convinced Cardinal Guidiccioni to reverse his position and approve the order, including the Five Chapters. The only qualification he placed was a limitation to sixty members, a restriction that would be abolished a decade later by Pope Julius III. Pope Paul III accepted the cardinal's recommendation, and on September 27, 1540, the Order of the Company of Jesus was established by Papal Bull, *Regimini Militantis Ecclesiae,* with slight modifications to the Formula.

Ignatius and Codure then set to work on the *Constitutions of the Society of Jesus,* which are the forty-nine articles that describe the organization of the order and the laws for its

Ignatius writes the Constitutions.

governance. After Codure's death in August 1541, Ignatius continued the effort. Expanding the Formula, the *Constitutions* specify a range of requirements in areas such as admission of candidates, formation, ordination, the office of the general, the teaching of catechism, and the establishment of colleges. Over the years they have served as a model for other men's and women's religious orders.

Despite his reluctance, the fifty-year-old Ignatius was chosen by his companions as the first head or superior general of the new community. He received all of the votes except for his own. Ignatius was so reluctant to accept the leadership that a second election was held, and he was again chosen. Still unwilling to accept the vote of his companions, Ignatius made a three-day retreat and a general confession similar to what he had done years earlier at Montserrat in Spain. His confessor advised him to accept the decision of his companions, for to do otherwise was to reject the Holy Spirit.

Those companions who were working in Rome made their religious professions on April 22, 1541, at a mass presided over by Ignatius, in the Chapel of Our Lady in the basilica of St. Paul Outside-the-Walls. The others, engaged in service outside of Rome, had to celebrate the good fortune of the new order from afar. Their own professions would be made later in the places where they were serving.

Many of the major religious orders have sister communities, such as the Franciscan order's Poor Clares. Unlike other orders, when the companions established the Society they did not include a sister order or female branch, an issue which was to plague the fledgling order. In 1542 Ignatius learned with misgivings that his long-time friend and benefactor, Isabel Roser, now widowed, planned to travel to Rome accompanied by two other women, all seeking to join a sister order. After a friendship of nearly twenty years' duration, Ignatius no doubt had some idea that Isabel would not easily adapt to religious life as he envisioned it. His fear was realized when the widow arrived laden with baggage. She required a full-time assistant, who for two years cleaned for her and waited on her. Isabel first stayed in a private home and then worked at the House of St. Martha which Ignatius had established for former prostitutes. Seeing Ignatius's resistance to the idea of a sister order, one of the women with Isabel gave up and was replaced by another. The women then petitioned the Holy Father for a sister order, which Pope Paul III ordered by decree. On December 25, 1545, the three women made their religious profession in the presence of Ignatius in the church of Santa Maria della Strada. Their vows, however, did little to stop Isabel from continuing the constant demands that she placed on Ignatius and the others. The problems escalated after she invited two of her nephews to Rome so she could help one of them find a wife. All of this was just too much for Ignatius who no longer wished to be distracted from the needs or mission of the Society. After deliberation, and with the authority of the pope, the women were dispensed from their vows. A repentant Isabel returned to Spain. Her friendship with Ignatius was eventually repaired and she apologized for the problems she had caused. Her religious commitment continued, however, as she founded an orphanage in Spain and, in 1550, entered a Franciscan convent in Barcelona.

After Ignatius's experience with Isabel Roser and the other women, he sought to ensure that the order would not again be confronted with the issue of including women. On May 20, 1547, Pope Paul IV responded to Ignatius's request that the Society be freed now and in the future from having authority over communities of women. Despite this, others were undeterred, including several prominent Spanish and Portuguese women. They sought admittance, appealing to various Jesuits as well as to Ignatius himself. Their requests, along with those of others, were denied.

The issue of women Jesuits would not easily fade away, and nearly a decade later it resurfaced in quite a formidable way. The prospective member this time was the powerful Juana d'Austria, second daughter of Charles V, Holy Roman Emperor, and great-granddaughter of Queen Isabella and King Ferdinand. At nineteen, newly widowed after the death of her seventeen-year-old husband, Prince John of Portugal, she left her infant son in Portugal and returned to Spain. In the absence of her brother, Philip II of Spain, who was in England with his wife, Mary Tudor, she served as regent from 1554–1559.

The independent and religiously-inclined Juana expressed interest in joining the Jesuits, rather than a sister order. Her request thrust the order into a dilemma, since either admitting or denying her would alienate someone. By admitting her, the Society risked angering her father or brother, who would be unhappy at her inability to remarry. But to do otherwise risked angering Juana herself. The situation was resolved by admitting her as a Jesuit. She would be bound by her vows, but the order could release her, if necessary. The entire matter was conducted in such a covert manner that her profession was made in secrecy. In correspondence she is referred to by the pseudonym Matteo Sánchez, and, following Ignatius's death, Montoya. She remained in her residence, dressing in secular clothes, although Ignatius expected her to contribute to the work of the order. She successfully defended the Society in Spain and contributed to its growth. She also founded a convent of Poor Clares in Madrid before her death in 1573 at the age of thirty-eight.

Why was Ignatius so opposed to the establishment of a sister order? Although women have been attracted to service and the religious life since the beginning of Christianity, Ignatius was not interested in including them in his new religious order. In responding to inquiries regarding the admittance of women, Ignatius gave some indication of his feelings on this delicate issue, suggesting that the conflicts taking place in convents would also affect a women's order in the Society. In several letters, he also wrote that the establishment of a women's community would impede the ability of members of the Society to travel anywhere they were needed, which is their primary mission. Since religious women were supposed to be cloistered, Ignatius did not envision them also placed at the service of the Holy Father.

With the order successfully established, Ignatius remained in Rome to oversee the Society, while the companions were sent to various places. He left Rome only a handful of times prior to his death in 1556. He spent much of his time working on the *Constitutions,* which took several years, and directing the others in their work, often through his letters. Ignatius left nearly seven thousand letters to church and government officials, family and friends, and to his companions; many of these letters were dictated to his secretary. Whether or not Ignatius's early days in the employ of Velázquez contributed to his views on correspondence, there is no question that he held firm ideas on the subject. As he wrote in December 1542 to Favre, and copied to the others, he expected each of them to write frequently, providing an accounting of their apostolic work. Ignatius would write a brief letter to them once a month and a more detailed one quarterly. The importance of Ignatius's letters cannot be overstated. They not only offer insights into the operation of the Society, but in their range of topics they provide a window into the first half of the sixteenth century.

Besides supervising the order, Ignatius initiated several ministries in Rome, which reflected his particular interests. These included an organization to distribute alms to the needy, a house for reformed prostitutes, a house for the daughters of prostitutes to provide them with an alternative way of life, and two houses for Jewish men and women catechumens.

The initial Formula approved by the pope experienced some changes over time, and a new draft was submitted to Pope Julius III for his approval. Among the changes were the pope's annulment of the earlier restriction limiting the order to sixty members and the inclusion of brothers (not priests) who would assist the priests. Approving the Formula, the pope issued the bull, *Exposcit debitum,* on July 21, 1550.

Ignatius had been asked to tell the story of his life and, after much convincing, he finally agreed. He related his story periodically over the course of two years to his assistant, Luis Gonçalves da Câmara, who was minister or house master of the Jesuit residence. This lengthy period was due to Ignatius's reluctance to share his private journey, his time-consuming involvement in the work of administering the Society, and the course of events, including the death of Pope Julius III. The story, known as the *Autobiography,* was finally concluded in 1555 because of the impending departure of Gonçalves da Câmara to Spain.

For much of Ignatius's adult life, he experienced poor health. His fasting and extreme penances resulted in debilitating stomach problems. Ignatius's death was not expected, although he had been ill for several months. He had overcome previous illnesses, so his companions were hopeful that he would survive his current sickness. While his secretary hastily rushed to the Vatican to receive a papal blessing from Pope Paul IV, as Ignatius desired, he died. The date was July 31, 1556, the eighth anniversary of papal approval of the *Spiritual Exercises.* He died at the order's residence in Rome, in the company of two Jesuits. Ignatius had received the grace of living to see the accomplishment of his great achievements, including the establishment of the Society of Jesus, papal approval of the *Spiritual Exercises,* and the completion of the *Constitutions.*

As word spread of Ignatius's death, enormous crowds gathered outside the residence. Many people wanted to touch him and possess a relic of the man whom they already believed to be a saint. For two days a public viewing was held in the church of Santa Maria della Strada which drew masses of people, many of whom sought a piece of his clothing or even of his flesh. The sick came seeking cures. Ignatius is said to have been the instrument of a miracle when a young girl was healed in the church after the sign of the cross was made over her with an item of clothing he had worn. Ignatius was first buried in this Jesuit church, but in 1587 his remains were reinterred in the new church of the Gesù in Rome.

For four years, beginning in 1605, Pope Paul V authorized the gathering of the miracles attributed to the intercession of Ignatius. Official statements were taken from nearly 1,600 witnesses, and more than 200 miracles were recognized. Ignatius was venerated by people from all walks of life. On July 27, 1609 he was beatified or declared blessed by Pope Paul V, and canonized by Pope Gregory XV on March 12, 1622. His feast day is celebrated on July 31, the day of his death.

CHAPTER TEN
THE LEGACY OF IGNATIUS OF LOYOLA: SERVICE AND SPIRITUALITY

Even before the new order was confirmed, the pope accepted the companions' offer of their services and made plans to send them on their first missions. Companions were initially sent to cities in Italy and were later sent to other countries. Since the companions vowed to go wherever they were most needed, the nature of their work was determined by their mission. For the most part, they continued the apostolic work they had engaged in when they had separated and traveled to the different Italian university cities. The companions gave the Spiritual Exercises, preached, administered the sacraments, and conversed with people whom they met. They also ministered to the sick and continued the practice of teaching catechism. In places experiencing the effects of the Reformation, they participated in discussions about Lutheranism.

Word spread throughout Europe of the companions' success and good work. Neighboring heads of state and bishops vied for the opportunity to have a companion or two toiling for them, not only in their own countries but also in faraway lands, such as India.

Companions attended some of the major theological events of the time: the Conference of Worms in 1540–1541, which met to discuss Catholic and Lutheran issues of faith; the Conference of Ratisbon in 1541, which continued the dialogue on disputed theological issues; and the Council of Trent, from 1545–1552, which reaffirmed traditional church teachings, such as the validity of seven sacraments, and introduced reforms, including the establishment of seminaries.

As new companions were attracted to the order, the Jesuits opened residences and colleges to house and educate them. The success of these endeavors led to the opening of colleges for other young men as well. In the years ahead, the order would be known worldwide for its educational apostolate. The establishment of the Collegio Romano, or Roman College, provided a classical curriculum modeled on the University of Paris. The school's name was later changed to the Gregorian University in honor of Pope Gregory XIII, who had endowed the college. The college became a center of theology in Rome.

By the time of Ignatius's death, the order had attracted nearly a thousand companions, and Jesuits were serving in missions in many countries. There were twelve provinces with houses and colleges in Portugal, Spain, India, Italy, and Brazil. These numbers were to increase substantially as the sixteenth century drew to a close. By the turn of the new century, there were more than 8,500 Jesuits in 23 provinces.

Today, Jesuits work in many places throughout the world—from medical facilities in Kenya to leprosy colonies in India, from barrios in Peru to Native American reservations in the United States. Jesuits have expanded their mission to serve the greater glory of God. They build schools and churches and work to spread the gospel. Jesuit priests and brothers minister in parishes, teach in high schools and universities, and write and perform research. They also work for social change and justice as lawyers, assist refugees, practice medicine in hospitals and clinics, run retreat houses, and minister in prisons.

Social justice, one of the church's social teachings, is especially important to the Society of Jesus. Members of the order work to educate people and to revise laws and institutions so that all of God's people will have access to the basic necessities of life including food, education, health care, housing, and employment. Jesuits are advocates for the poor and the oppressed and are committed to ending injustice.

In 1995 over two hundred delegates representing Jesuit provinces worldwide assembled in Rome. This congregation met to decide on future apostolate work and endeavors of the order. In the document "Cooperation with the Laity in Mission" (Decree Thirteen), the Society recognized the large number of laypeople who have been called to ministry since the 1960s. The Jesuits pledged to cooperate with the laity in the fulfillment of their own mission by "sharing our spiritual and apostolic inheritance, our educational resources, and our friendship." Together with the laity, the Jesuits continue the mission of service begun by Ignatius of Loyola more than four centuries ago.

The service of the Jesuits grows from their spirituality, which originated in the experiences of Ignatius in his conversion. His realization of God's love for him resulted in a desire to return that love. He chose to show his love for God through a life of service to God's people.

ST. IGNATIUS OF LOYOLA

Ignatius's spirituality is especially present in his writings, all of which reveal his desire to find God's will and follow it. A major component of Ignatian spirituality is discernment—the ability to determine what God's will or plan is for oneself. Throughout our lives, we are continually called on to make choices and decisions. Discernment enables us to make these decisions in agreement with what God wants us to do. As Ignatius recovered from his injuries and reflected on his readings, he noticed that certain feelings brought him deep peace or happiness or consolation, while others had the opposite effect. They brought him short-lived happiness or left him sad or desolate. Ignatius was beginning to understand the way God leads us through our human feelings. Those that left him happy or content indicated God's favor. A major part of engaging in the Spiritual Exercises is to discern who God is calling the person to be.

Most people who undertook the Exercises in Ignatius's lifetime benefited in some way from the experience. Some, like the masters of Paris, chose to make profound changes in their lives. They gave up their planned academic careers and material goods to serve God. Others desired to live their lives in closer accord with the Gospels. Today's retreatants, or people who make a retreat, are no less affected by their experience. They too desire to make changes in their own lives.

As originally envisioned by Ignatius, the Exercises are a thirty-day retreat divided into four weeks. Each week has a different theme. The First Week focuses on creation, sin, and death. Week Two emphasizes Jesus's life and ministry; the week contains an important meditation on the Kingdom of Christ (where the retreatant desires to serve and imitate Christ), and the Two Standards (good and evil or God and Satan). Week Three concentrates on the Passion, while

Week Four explores the mystery of the Resurrection and Ascension. To enable greater numbers of people to benefit from the Exercises, they are adapted to the needs of the participants. Many lay people are unable to take the full thirty-day retreat because of family, work, or school commitments. Annotation Nineteen, one of twenty introductory notes to the *Exercises,* recognizes the gifts and needs of the laity and provides instructions for making the "Retreat in Daily Life." This annotation enables a retreatant to participate in the Exercises without leaving his or her own environment. Retreatants partake in the Exercises on a part-time basis over consecutive weeks. Either individually or in a group, retreatants meet with a director and pray a set amount of time each day.

Regardless of how the Exercises are organized, their goal has remained unchanged throughout the centuries. The retreatants learn to see God actively working in their own lives. The Exercises help them discover how much God loves them and what God's plan is for them. As a result, they grow closer to God. At the conclusion of the Exercises, retreatants frequently are led to some type of service out of gratitude for God's love. They may ask themselves: What can I do for my community and my church? How can I help my family? What can I do to improve my school or my job environment? Possible forms of service include helping the sick and suffering, aiding the marginalized—those that are not included in the mainstream of society, or working to change unjust social structures and conditions. Just like Ignatius's first companions, each of us has the ability to respond to our unique call to build God's reign.

Ignatian spirituality includes several different types of prayer including oral or formulated prayer, reflected prayer, meditation, and contemplation. Oral or formulated prayer involves slowly reciting out loud the words to a set prayer such as the Our Father. Reflected prayer involves reading scripture or other spiritual works and thinking about the meaning of what is read. In meditation, one thinks quietly with the goal of understanding or figuring something out. Meditation reaches a much deeper level than regular studying by always keeping God in mind. In contemplation, one mentally enters a scene, usually from the Gospels.

As an example of contemplation, consider the story of Jesus's birth in Luke's Gospel. Begin by first reading the scripture passage several times and then closing your eyes to visualize the setting. Now picture yourself in the story, and act out the role of one of the characters by using your imagination and five senses (seeing, hearing, smelling, tasting, and feeling) to bring the narrative to life. Supply any missing details or parts to the story. Ask yourself questions to enter the scene more fully. What is it like to be Mary, who at fourteen is about to give birth to her first child? Far from home, she is traveling on a donkey to an unfamiliar town. Is she tired, worried, or frightened? And Joseph? Where will his family find shelter? Is he nervous or afraid? Are there other people on their journey? Do they stop and talk to anyone? What do they say? What do they hear? What are the roads like? Flat, winding, hilly? What are the weather conditions? Is it hot, cold, rainy, dusty, windy? Or take the role of one of the animals, perhaps the donkey. Is the donkey tired, hungry, thirsty? Are the donkey's legs sore? What is it like to carry Mary who will soon give birth to Jesus? What is it like to be present at the birth of Jesus?

Another method of prayer which is important to Ignatian spirituality is known as the *examen*. This prayer is performed daily. The examen involves reviewing the activities and people encountered during the day to determine God's presence or absence. Where was God present in your day? Was God in the telephone call or letter that came from someone you had not heard from in a long time? Did you do something today that you were unable to do before? Did you receive a kind word from a teacher, an employer, a stranger? Where was God absent today? Was there any moment when you felt totally alone, as if God had abandoned you? Then, reflect on the feelings you had during these moments. Share these feelings with God in dialogue. Continue the conversation and listen to how God responds to you.

While the examen and the other types of prayer can each be used individually, they are all found in the *Spiritual Exercises*. The contribution of Ignatius's *Spiritual Exercises* is enormous. In 1922, in recognition of their contribution, Pope Pius XI named Ignatius patron saint of retreats and spiritual exercises. Today they are given and used by men and women of many religious traditions throughout the world.

One of the key defining characteristics of Ignatian Spirituality is Ignatius's ability to find God in all things. God can be found everywhere in daily life, whether at home or work, school or play, or worship. If we look we can find God in the people and ordinary events of our lives, including our relatives, friends, and even strangers—and in the many activities and encounters that we have.

Grounded in the vision of Ignatius, Jesuits today continue to embrace their founder's spirituality of service. By proclaiming the gospel, reconciling and healing, teaching, giving the Spiritual Exercises, and being companions to each other and for others, they walk in the footsteps of the first companions.

ST. IGNATIUS OF LOYOLA

Ignatius's injuries during the Battle of Pamplona led to his period of forced quiet and reflection, which greatly influenced not only him, but ultimately the world as well. This man who was just over five feet tall left a legacy much bigger than he and more permanent than his dreams. By placing his trust in God he overcame countless adversities including perilous travel conditions, inclement weather, imprisonment, the plague, and debilitating illness to attain his desired goals. From his beginnings as a street preacher and teacher in Spain, Ignatius's gift to people the world over continues today. Never looking back, Ignatius of Loyola left his family home, not to seek his fortune, but rather to surrender it to the service of God and the church.

BIBLIOGRAPHY

Works by and about St. Ignatius of Loyola

The Autobiography of St. Ignatius Loyola with Related Documents. Translated by Joseph F. O'Callaghan. Edited with introduction and notes by John C. Olin. New York: Harper & Row, 1974.

Bartoli, Daniel, S.J. *History of the Life and Institute of St. Ignatius de Loyola, Founder of the Society of Jesus.* 2 vols. New York: P. J. Kenedy, 1855.

Brodrick, James, S.J. *Saint Ignatius Loyola: The Pilgrim Years.* London: Burns & Oats, 1956.

Caraman, Philip, S.J. *Ignatius Loyola: A Biography of the Founder of the Jesuits.* San Francisco: Harper & Row, 1990.

Dalmases, Cándido de, S.J. *Ignatius of Loyola, Founder of the Jesuits: His Life and Work.* Translated by Jerome Aixalá, S.J. St. Louis: Institute of Jesuit Sources, 1985.

Guibert, Joseph de, S.J. *The Jesuits: Their Spiritual Doctrine and Practice. A Historical Study.* Translated by William J. Young, S.J. Chicago: Institute of Jesuit Sources, 1964.

ST. IGNATIUS OF LOYOLA

Lacouture, Jean. *Jesuits: A Multibiography*. Translated by Jeremy Leggatt. Washington, D.C.: Counterpoint, 1995.

Letters of St. Ignatius of Loyola. Selected and translated by William J. Young, S.J. Chicago: Loyola University, 1959.

McCarthy, John L., S.J., editor. *Documents of the Thirty-Fourth General Congregation of the Society of Jesus*. St. Louis: Institute of Jesuit Sources, 1995.

Meissner, W. W., S.J., M.D. *Ignatius of Loyola: The Psychology of a Saint*. New Haven: Yale University, 1992.

Padberg, John, S.J. "Secret, Perilous Project." *Company, a Magazine of the American Jesuits* 17 (Fall 1999): 28–29.

A Pilgrim's Journey: The Autobiography of Ignatius Loyola. Introduction, Translation, and Commentary by Joseph N. Tylenda, S.J. Wilmington: Michael Glazier, 1989.

Prescott, H. F. M. *Jerusalem Journey: Pilgrimage to the Holy Land in the Fifteenth Century*. London: Eyre & Spottiswoode, 1954.

Rahner, Hugo, S.J. *Saint Ignatius Loyola: Letters to Women*. Translated by Kathleen Pond and S. A. H. Weetman. New York: Herder and Herder, 1960.

Saint Ignatius of Loyola: The Constitutions of the Society of Jesus. Translated, with an Introduction and a Commentary by George E. Ganss, S.J. St. Louis: Institute of Jesuit Sources, 1970.

St. Ignatius' Own Story: As Told to Luis González de Cámara. With a sampling of his letters. Translated by

William J. Young, S.J. Chicago: Henry Regnery, 1956. Reprint. Chicago: Loyola University, 1980.

The Spiritual Diary of St. Ignatius, February 2, 1544 to February 27, 1545. Translated by William J. Young, S.J. Reprinted from *Woodstock Letters*, 1958. Rome: Centrum Ignatianum Spiritualitatis, 1979.

Tellechea Idígoras, José Ignacio. *Ignatius of Loyola: The Pilgrim Saint*. Translated, edited, and with a preface by Cornelius Michael Buckley, S.J. Chicago: Loyola University, 1994.

Tylenda, Joseph N., S.J. "The Books that Led Ignatius to God." *Review for Religious* 57 (May-June 1998): 286–98.

Other Works Consulted

Browning, W. R. F. *A Dictionary of the Bible*. Oxford: Oxford University, 1997.

Collins, Roger. *The Basques*. Second Edition. Cambridge, Mass.: Basil Blackwell, 1990.

Cross, F. L., editor. *The Oxford Dictionary of the Christian Church*. Third edition edited by E. A. Livingstone. Oxford: Oxford University Press, 1997.

Kendall, Alan. *Medieval Pilgrims*. New York: G. P. Putnam's Sons, 1970.

Kilgallen, John J., S.J. *A New Testament Guide to the Holy Land*. Second Edition. Chicago: Loyola, 1998.

Kurlansky, Mark. *The Basque History of the World*. New York: Walker & Company, 1999.

Llopis, Manuel Martínez. "Spain and Portugal." In *Royal Cookbook: Favorite Court Recipes from the World's Royal Families*, 102–15. New York: Parents' Magazine, 1971.

McKendrick, Melveena. *Ferdinand and Isabella*. New York: American Heritage, 1968.

———. *The Horizon Concise History of Spain*. New York: American Heritage, 1972.

Montguerre, Jean-Marc [Jean-Marc Langlois-Berthelot]. *St. Francis Xavier*. Translated by Ruth Murdoch. Garden City, N.Y.: Doubleday, 1963.

Murphy-O'Connor, Jerome, O.P. *The Holy Land: An Archaeological Guide from Earliest Times to 1700*. Fourth Edition. Oxford: Oxford University Press, 1998.

New Catholic Encyclopedia. 15 vols. and 4 supplements. New York: McGraw-Hill, 1967.

Walsh, Michael, editor. *Butler's Lives of the Saints*. Concise Edition. Revised & Updated. San Francisco: HarperCollins, 1991.

Wareham, Norman, and Jill Gill. *Shrines of the Holy Land: A Pilgrim's Travel Guide*. Rev. edition. Liguori, Mo.: Liguori, 1998.

Wilson, Colin. *The Atlas of Holy Places and Sacred Sites*. New York: DK Publishing, 1996.